DESERT NURSE

DESERT NURSE

BETTY C. PARKIN

ROBERT HALE · LONDON

Robert Hale Limited
Clerkenwell House
Clerkenwell Green
London EC1R 0HT

Photoset in North Wales by
Derek Doyle & Associates, Mold, Clwyd.
Printed in Great Britain by
WBC Print Ltd., Barton Manor, Bristol.
Bound by WBC Bookbinders Limited.

Contents

Illustrations

Life is eternal; and love is immortal;
and death is only a horizon; and a horizon
is nothing save the limit of our sight.
                    BISHOP THOMAS BRETT

Introduction: *Strings*

The hospital matron's office seemed as cold and unfriendly as the words she was speaking as my aunt and I faced the stern lady across her oak desk.

My thoughts strayed momentarily as I wondered what would happen if she took a really deep breath. Would the buttons marching so proudly down her blue uniform dress snap off one by one? While the small muslin bows quivered beneath her ample chin? When I'm old, really old, I mentally emphasized, shall I wear bows like that? From the ignorance of my seventeen years I could not know that in the nursing profession they are called 'strings', not bows.

Her voice brought me back to reality.

'You have indeed wasted my time and your money by coming here.' Matron turned her steely eyes towards my aunt, who had accompanied me on this, my first interview, in 1928. 'And you, my good woman, I would have credited you with more sense than to bring me a girl with a stammer. Accept her as a probationer nurse?' Matron's voice rose at least two tones with sheer disbelief. 'And have every young patient imitating her impediment? Oh, dear me, no! Children pick up bad habits readily enough without the need to rattle them against their ears.' She shuffled some loose papers on her desk into a precise pile in front of her. 'Good-day to you both; and close the door as you go out, please.'

I gulped with deep disappointment. Nursing was the only career I had ever cared about. I couldn't, I wouldn't, have my entire future and my girlhood dreams smashed by this woman. I'd make it, whatever she said, and I'd prove her wrong if it took all my life to do so.

Aunt and I boarded a tram not far from the tall iron hospital gates through which I had entered with such anticipation only to leave with a heavy step and an equally heavy heart; and my aunt's anger did nothing to help matters.

'To speak like that! To me! Why, I have never treated a maid – no, not even my charwoman – so rudely. And it is all your fault. We have been patient with you, tried in every way to distract you from this foolish idea of nursing, but no ... you would not listen to anyone.'

I knew better than to argue. I looked out of the tram window, watching our change of scene as the vehicle jerked us from the East End streets towards South London. And still my aunt kept up her tirade.

'Now see what's come of it! You've never been a strong child. Goodness knows what germs you may have picked up already in that ... that place. Oh, do sit up, girl, and blow your nose, and please try not to make an exhibition of yourself.'

I gazed down the near-empty tram then and thought I'd need to stand on my head to have that effect. The grey water of the Thames as we moved along the Embankment matched my depressing mood, while my hopes for the career I had so believed I could follow were dwindling with every yard we travelled. If I couldn't be a nurse, what else was there for me to achieve?

As the tram followed a sharp bend in the road and the few passengers lurched in reaction, the thin, watery sun trickled through the branches of the riverside tree. It was only a little sunshine but it was enough. I flung up my head defiantly.

One day ... one day I too would wear those muslin bows.

Modern teaching would have us believe that my stammer was due to my strange upbringing.

It did not seem strange to me, for I remember my childhood as a happy time.

My mother, having had an extremely difficult time at

my birth, was advised not to have more children – this when Caesarean births were very rare. My father was a lively, active man who had suffered from severe deafness following a childhood illness. Any normal speech was very difficult for him, though he went through life in his own way quite happily, and my mother cared for him in her own lethargic fashion.

Soon after I was born they took a small corner shop in South London. My mother found that the care of a very small, premature baby took all her time, and with her poor health and my father's handicap I cannot imagine the shop could ever have been very successful.

When I was three years old, my mother became pregnant again and even more languid and tired.

My father was the youngest of a family of nine, and it was the custom at times of illness and distress for children to be sent to Uncle Basil and Aunt Nellie, whose large house had room for them. Uncle Basil was the oldest brother, and his wife was fond of little girls and had maids to help her, so I was sent to them. There were two girl cousins much older than me, one already working as a civil servant, the other still a schoolgirl. The older one took me to church and taught me hymns; the younger, in true schoolgirl contempt, called me 'that child'.

My brother arrived in due course but, being a very large baby and my mother extremely short, his birth was again a very difficult one. Mother remained in poor health and was able to do little but care for him. Meanwhile, as I had settled down happily, I remained with my aunt and uncle, my cousins and a devoted maid. Whenever my return home was mentioned, there was always a holiday, a nursery class at school or something else to put it off until my mother's health had improved, for she still remained delicate.

I did not find it unusual, as my friend lived with her grandma – her parents were abroad; another friend was orphaned and she lived with her aunt. In days when so many middle-class folk had posts overseas – in the Empire – and when the death of young parents was not uncommon, many children spent part of their lives with relatives. I thought I was very lucky having two homes. I adored my uncle, who, if he could not answer one of my questions, would bring me back a book from the shop the very next evening.

By the time I was ready for grammar school, my parents had given up their shop and had decided to move out of London to the suburbs on the edge of Kent. My father had gone into the family bookshop. 'When we are settled,' my mother said, 'you must come home to live.' But the move upset her, and I had become settled in a grammar school, and my aunt said, 'You must understand, your mother's health is not good – she will always be delicate.'

Part of my holidays were spent in Kent. My brother and I enjoyed each other's company (and in later years became very close), and so my mother continued in her own quiet way.

My schoolgirl cousin lost her superior attitude towards me and became engrossed in her medical career, and I said quite firmly 'I am going to be a nurse.'

From where came this urgent desire to nurse? Try as I will, I cannot recall. Perhaps it was sheer obstinacy that, after that first rebuff and the many arguments of teachers, family and well-meaning friends, I still pursued the idea, stammer and all.

Relatives just haven't a clue. They thought of me always as a quiet, well-behaved child and found it hard to appreciate that the shy girl was fast becoming a determined adult.

Then fate played into my hands. The matron of the hospital to which I next applied had just retired, and her successor, slim, young and elegant, seemed as nervous as the candidate as she conducted her first interview. She never mentioned my stammer. But then, surprisingly, I almost forgot it myself.

I came out of her room and crossed the gleaming black and white tiles of the hospital hallway, my head in a daze. I had done it. Only the stiff paper in my hand seemed real, and that was the official signed permission to purchase my hospital uniform.

1 *'Hey! We've got a new nurse!'*

The first person to address me as 'Nurse' was a faded dressmaker in a badly washed woollen jacket. She glanced at the well-corseted figure of my aunt (of course, I hadn't been allowed to attend this, or any other, interview unchaperoned), then weighed up the cost of aunt's black corded silk coat and dusted the chair for her to sit down. I have reason to remember and to bless that coat, for throughout the years in which I went there to purchase uniforms, that same dressmaker never failed to enquire after my aunt's health. 'Such a well-dressed lady' was her routine remark, and she would accept from me less than half the deposit demanded from my companions; providing uniform dresses, caps and aprons wasn't easy on a salary of £20 a year.

That first measuring will remain for ever in my mind. The small sitting-room of the dressmaker's house reeked with the special smell of cotton material, while the green and striped stiff dresses hung from a brass rail. As I undressed for my measurements to be taken, the dresses and the bales of cotton seemed to encircle me, like a symbol of authority and of the confining years ahead.

On my first day I had to report to Home Sister. She was small and so neat as to make me think of a model in a shop window. She handed me a key and an equally neat and concise statement.

'Sixteen articles only to be displayed, including your toilet requisites,' she announced sternly. 'Your bed is to be completely stripped before going on duty and remade in the morning break, when you will also mop and dust your room. Nothing is allowed to be hung on the walls.' With a grim face, she then turned on her heel and left me.

I looked around me. This is no larger than a horse-box, I reflected. Although I knew nothing whatever of horses or their requirements, I couldn't liken this cell-like room to anything else.

My new home had once been a high-ceilinged ward and had been converted into cubicles, four on each side of a central passage divided by six-foot high, green-painted partitions. A bed, a chest of drawers, a cupboard and a hard wooden chair completed the furniture. A small rug looked like an island on the gleaming polished floor. This was my bedroom, my hospital 'home' for the next 3½ years. The 'room' had a window with a huge ventilator and reminded me of draughty schoolrooms. It looked out onto a grim courtyard and a small windowless building. I later learned that this was the mortuary.

I unpacked my belongings and waited until there was a knock upon my door, and a young face peered around the opening. 'I have to take you to supper. Come on, quickly; we're late already.'

The girl was breathless, her cap askew, and there were damp patches on her crumpled apron. She had none of the serene deportment with which I had pictured my future nursing colleagues. A faint aroma clung to her: a mixture of baby food, powder and disinfectant.

'There is no sister at supper,' the girl panted as we hurried down the stairs. 'But, remember, you must stand up whenever a senior comes into the dining-room, even if you are eating.'

Along corridors, down more stairs, around corners and eventually we entered a dimly lit basement, where a few nurses, who were sitting at a long wooden table, looked at me curiously and then, without even a 'hello', went on with their meal. A plate of tasteless shepherd's pie and a cup of weak tea were given to me. I looked around for an alternative choice but there was nothing else to eat but a slice of dry bread.

Conversation seemed slight, I thought, for a group of young girls. I had yet to learn that, after eleven hours of arduous duty, there was little energy left for chatter.

When the meal was finished, my guide hurried me back upstairs. 'I have to show you how to make up your cap,' she said with a heavy sigh, 'and I do want an early bath, then it's your turn. But don't take longer than ten minutes in the bathroom or the next in the queue will be banging on the door. We're all tired and we have to be in our rooms by ten o'clock sharp.'

Later, as I lay in my bed, I heard swift footsteps and the rustle of an apron. '10.30, nurses,' came a quiet, hissing voice. 'All lights out now.'

There was a click of switches, and the cubicles darkened. Beside me, my new uniform glimmered faintly and the stiff white apron lay beside the cap, which was just a triangle of stiffly starched linen and had to be tied in a very strange fashion next morning.

I was eighteen years old. And tomorrow ... yes, tomorrow I was to become a probationer nurse.

The same worried-looking girl took me to my ward next morning. 'Staff Nurse is off,' she confided. 'That means that Sister will be on duty all day, worse luck. Isn't it just *my* luck to get you, brand new, to assist me? We'll never get done, I can tell you that now. We'll be running late all day.'

This was not the most encouraging of remarks with which to start my career. But I was not dismayed, even after the breakfast of lumpy porridge and tinned herrings. Tinned herrings at 6.30 and not yet daylight? Bread and marge would have to suffice for me, if that was the standard breakfast.

'Don't just stand there. Take off your cuffs.'

I was pushed into a cupboard-like room beside a toilet, and as I struggled to get out of the stiff wristlets I was wishing I could also take off the starched collar which was already chafing my neck. Then I went into the ward.

Children's voices called out cheerily from twelve cots, spaced evenly against the tiled walls. A fire crackled behind a tall nursery fireguard. I felt quite surprised that there was none of the awed hush or moaning cries that I had anticipated.

Most of those children are but blurred memories, and yet two remain so clearly in my memory. One was a tiny baby whose distorted nose and mouth were coated with a black substance through which poked the ends of stitches. I guessed the wee mite had met with an accident, not realizing I was seeing a problem of the future – the care of post-operative 'harelip' babies.

The other child stared at me, and stared again, before a wide smile spread over his sharp Cockney face. 'Hey! We've got a new nurse!' he called to his sick colleagues, with the wisdom of his seven years and a week or so as a hospital patient. 'I'll bet you're brand new!' he shrilled. 'You won't know nuffin'. Cor ... Sister won't 'arf 'ave a time wiv you.' And for the rest of his stay in hospital that child plagued me every minute of his day.

Why, I wondered, did I have to start my career on a Sunday? I was soon to find out ...

'There's no ward maid today, so you'll have to sweep,' Nurse cried as she dashed past me, washbowl in hand.

My efforts on the kitchen floor at home had always seemed quite successful, but here, with a huge brush, the dust pirouetted around, behind but never beneath the bristles.

'You can't do it. You've left another lot of fluff. Coo ... look at yer. Sister won't 'arf tell you off.' The wretched 7-year-old chanted incessantly until there came an added descant from the nurse.

'Pull the cots right out. Scrape the fluff from the wheels with that old knife. Oh, for Heaven's sake,' she exploded, 'put the broom away. There's the windowsills and all the locker tops to be washed yet.' Her tone left me in no doubt that my assistance was not of the highest standard. And I'd hoped that she might be my friend!

I followed her demonstration of kicking the wheels into a straight line while my expensive regulation shoes (laced-up 'Oxfords' with a stipulated height of heel) received the first of their daily scuffs, before my senior companion stopped abruptly.

'Oh, it'll have to do,' she muttered with unconcealed exasperation and then gasped, 'Oh, the flowers!'

The swing doors clashed behind her, and when she reappeared she was clutching two vases. With a deft movement she whipped from them several faded blooms and, to my amazement, stuffed them behind the bib of her apron.

It was a long time before I realized how fortunate I had been with my first ward sister. Sister Lake was a large woman – large in every way. Warm-hearted, Irish – and very proud of it too, she was known as one of the 'hospital characters', her strong personality overshadowing those of her more conventional colleagues. They raised their eyebrows when her hearty laughter echoed through the corridors or when, in the nurses' home or sisters' quarters perhaps, her voice trilled above the sound of her sewing machine as she 'did a small job' for herself or, indeed, anyone in need, pedalling away on the noisy old treadle. Most of this sewing was in making brightly coloured dresses for her annual holidays. The tightly fitting uniform restricted her ample figure but not her laughter, nor the flash of her merry dark eyes. In moments of crises she was a Junoesque figure, and only the odd strands of black hair escaping from the thick coils beneath the cap denoted her anxieties.

From the beginning, I admired her sense of justice. No careless work went unnoticed, no slipshod care of a tiny child escaped reprimand, but equally, an achievement of skill or effort was readily rewarded by a word of praise, an encouraging smile, a quick joke.

It was from Sister Lake that I gained a fanciful idea of Death, which was to remain with me throughout my hospital days. I learned that Death was no shadowy figure. Rather was he an interloper skulking in a corner of every ward waiting for opportunity, waiting for my attention to wander, so that he could sneak in and snatch away a sick child.

Thinking back, I know this idea grew from the first time I saw Sister Lake carrying a new patient into the ward. A small and very sick baby. The waiting cot was pushed near to the fire, screened from draughts, the baby wrapped in a warm blanket, and then Sister Lake rolled up her sleeves and started the treatment. The fight for the baby's life had begun.

During my years of early training I had no need to alter my sleeves. They were always fastened above my elbows ready for action and, following her example, I too could tighten my lips and step with purpose.

'Compassion' was not a word in common use then, but compassion was what those dedicated nursing ladies had. Those ward sisters whose lives were bounded by hospital walls and long hours of duty, rewarded by salaries of just £70 per year.

From those ladies, we probationers and nurses learned that babies, however tiny, have their individual hold on life. Some, with even minor problems, find the world too overwhelming to make an effort to survive, while others, with everything stacked against them, battle on and struggle through. Are these the ones destined for great events, these brave ones? Are they to become 'names' that others will notice? Slowly I learnt to recognize them and then to turn and glare into the corner of the ward and mutter to my imaginary enemy, 'This one is not for you.' In the days before the common use of incubators, heart machines and even antibiotics, I struggled with them against prematurity and pneumonia and learnt to recognize and admire those tiny fighters.

Days passed swiftly. Too fast for all the menial tasks that made up our time. Washing and polishing the oak trays that slid noisily up and down the cot rails. Cleaning lockers, scrubbing instruments and bed mackintoshes; and sluicing, day after day after day, the endles piles of babies' napkins.

'Did you say "napkins", Nurse?' Sister's voice registered mild horror. 'We never use that word here. They are known as "Sundries".'

Whatever they were to be called, they were still the curse of each young nurse. Wet ones to be counted, the numbers added to those in use, plus those in the cupboard. Together they had to reach the allocation for the ward. Frequently they did not, but there was never time to check the figures, hurriedly scribbled in the crumpled notebook, for at 7.50 p.m. precisely a senior sister handed out replacements on the third floor of the hospital. Prior to this allocation, the buckets of wet ones had been carried down to the basement.

This was the time when those cold stairs became purgatory for me. Most nurses slept with the foot of their beds raised to ease their aching feet. Not me. I needed a pillow under my legs to try to ease the inexplicable ache of my knees.

Those stairs! Shallow steps of polished wood, they haunted me by day and by night, for the lift could be used only by doctors or if the sick child to be carried was over three years old. The stairs were in the care of one elderly woman who, on her knees, waxed and polished them daily, from the fourth floor down to the tiled entrance hall. She rarely raised her head as we passed and repassed her. Sometimes I would mutter a cheery 'good-morning' to the Stair Lady but she never answered, and if she had a name I can no longer recall it, yet the stairs and the woman are clear pictures in my memory.

Ward maids were an added terror, often more of a problem than the current ward sister. Small and thin, they were frequently the product of an orphanage whose matron had decided that their disposition was not pleasant enough for private domestic work and had steered them instead to a further institution. Perhaps as an act of revenge for their lot, they bullied us unmercifully and, as the one ward maid looked after the ward sister also, many a nurse had her personal report spoiled by sly hints slipped in with the coffee tray.

'If the crocks aren't out in five minutes ... five minutes I say ...' a raucous voice would call as I struggled single-handed to feed a ward of babies and toddlers, 'I shan't wash 'em up.' And it was no idle threat. Or, 'Which nurse has spilled water on *My floor*?' came a frequent irate cry as we dashed around with the changing trolley.

Floors! They shone with a brilliance never seen these days. They were the downfall of many nurses, patients and visitors. Yet their impeccable shine was the recognized symbol of a good ward sister and her cherished ward maid.

I had been a nurse for about eight months when one morning I was told I had to leave the ward at 2 p.m. so that I could report for night duty that evening. In my lunch break I moved my belongings to the top floor, into a 'real' room on the night corridor, whose entrance door was locked at noon. The thought of night duty did not alarm me, but at that time I did not know I would find it the most rewarding part of my work. Something about the dimly lit wards and the sleeping children made an instant appeal to me. The ward was ... mine, although of course Night Sister visited frequently and could always be reached quickly by telephone.

Night Sister was a tall, angular woman, thin-faced, with sparse black hair screwed up into a tight bun. The rustle of her starched apron always preceded her quick footsteps as she hurried, head poking forward as if keeping in line with the awkward carriage of an arm broken in her childhood and badly set. She was a woman of infinite curiosity. No hospital secret escaped her, and she was much given to favouritism among her staff. The daughter of a country vicar and full of technical and nursing knowledge, she still remained quite naïve and seemingly untouched by worldly affairs and completely absorbed in her strange night life.

The worst part of this duty was the food. We were always hungry and always waiting for, or bringing back, parcels of fruit, cake and chocolate from home. My family also supplemented the meagre weekly allowance of metal polish and cleaning powder, for between my twelve-hour stint of watching, feeding and toileting twelve or more children aged from birth to ten years, I had to clean and polish the brasses. They were the doorplates and commemorative plaques over the cots, desk equipment, cupboard and door handles and the copper instrument-sterilizer. No matter how many admissions, operations or deaths happened in the night hours, the brasses must still reach the requisite standard by next morning. Washing bowls, toothmugs, towelhooks were all the night nurses' responsibility, and keeping them gleaming was quite impossible with the small amount of cleanser put into a rusty tin and marked with a dirty label 'Night Nurse Only'.

For reasons quite unknown to me, I became one of Night Sister's 'Blue Eyes', and because of this I found myself promoted from the small surgical ward, in which I cared for hernias, appendices and harelipped babies, into the smaller ward for very tiny infants.

Incubators were not as yet in common use, although there were a few scattered around the country in experimental hospitals. Eight small white cots with hanging draperies swung gently, and within them were eight near-skeleton babies weighing only two to four pounds each. A betting man would not, I think, have laid great odds on their survival, but then, in all my eighteen years of life, I had not known a betting man.

I had as yet only seen but not touched death, and it was ten o'clock at night when the first baby in my care passed away. Night Sister rustled in with the doctor, and when he had gone, we knelt and said the prayer for 'this, our last act of love'. Sister moved away, muttering that the hospital was busy and that I could manage, as she had to report to theatre for an emergency operation. Her starched apron rustled again and she was gone.

I did what had to be done. The tiny shroud, the label and the posy of flowers placed between the minute hands. Next I had to change, feed and turn the seven other infants in my care, and only then, hesitant and unhappy, I put on my cloak before lifting up my tiny and so light burden.

The ward door closed behind me, shutting out the warmth of the crackling fire and the rosy glow of the shaded lamp. For an instant, from the floor above came a brightness and noise as the theatre door opened and a trolley trundled through. The light lasted only an instant, and then before me lay the dark well of the staircase, the pale steps leading through pools of darkness down to the black and white tiles of the entrance hall gleaming like a river below. Carefully, reverently, I walked down further with my small, fondly held bundle.

The porter had unlocked the courtyard door, switched

on a light. With my free hand I pulled my cloak closer against the shivering chill creeping over me. Death had not as yet led me through that door on the opposite side of the cobbled yard. Then I took a deep breath and pushed the door wide.

Beneath a coloured mosaic on the wall – which stated 'Suffer Little Children to Come Unto Me' – stood two vases of flowers. Since then, white tulips have always had a very special meaning for me.

Tearfully, reluctantly, I laid the tiny body on the cold marble slab. I was unwilling to leave my little patient and added a whispered 'God bless you.' I would have liked to stay awhile, but I was on duty, so I turned the key in the door and hurried back to my living babies.

By 3 a.m. the stripped, cleaned and remade cot was occupied by an hour-old baby boy brought in by a district midwife. I was watching him as I sat by the fire to eat my 'afternoon tea', which had been brought to me by another junior nurse.

'Rather you than me,' she said, pouring out the tea and handing me two slices of bread and marge. 'This ward would give me the creeps even though I am run off my feet. Sorry there's nothing else. I tell you, we shall all die of starvation before we finish our training.'

'Don't speak of dying here,' I retorted swiftly and a little angrily. 'Just look at that little mite, just been admitted. He's just *got* to survive.'

It was nearly daylight when I walked across the courtyard again, to where the tulips still glimmered coldly and the wind blew as chill. The 'enemy' had beaten me again. But I was going to win the next battle. I was determined.

The same junior nurse was awaiting my return to the ward, a large bundle in her arms. 'Night Sister says you have a lodger. There's an emergency coming in to us, so Harry here is going home at nine this morning. Aren't you, my pet?' she added fondly. 'He's been bathed but not fed. Here ...' She thrust the baby, some charts and a bottle into my hands.

Round, pink and dimpled, he stared up at the bottle.

Noisily and hungrily he attacked it, his little firm limbs kicking against me in his eagerness. I burped him, not even caring when he spilled a little on my collar, because I so wanted to enjoy his happiness. There was scarcely room for his plump body in the tiny emergency cradle, and he laughed as it creaked with the movement of his vigorous kicking. I laughed too, in gratitude for the robust health of him.

In later years there were more walks across courtyards but never have the flowers gleamed so white, never the winds felt so chill as on that night in my first year of training.

The prophecies of my family came true. I did catch nearly everything. Scarlet fever came to me when I had completed my three months on night duty. The fever was slight, but the complications – three attacks of quinsies – were much worse. I felt very ill indeed.

At the end of eight weeks my own doctor still considered me unfit to work among sick patients, but the hospital authorities thought otherwise. The matron's letter was emphatic: unless I returned to duty that week, my training would be terminated. Of course, I returned to work. I wasn't going to let anyone stop my training now, so against the advice of the 'family doctor' I reported for duty, and for the next five months I worked on medical wards and fell victim to every cold and sore throat that came my way.

Each time I suffered, Home Sister regarded my condition as due entirely to my negligence. Either I had or had not taken sufficient exercise in the fresh air; or I must have opened or shut my bedroom windows incorrectly. Finally I was despatched to keep an appointment at a nearby general hospital to be examined by an ear, nose and throat consultant. He signed me 'off duty', as a 'menace to society', and arranged for me to be admitted to his wards for intensive treatment prior to the removal of my tonsils.

Home Sister's reaction to this information was a genteel but pronounced sniff before she said, 'They must have plenty of staff in that place if nurses are put off duty and kept off duty at the slightest excuse. You will please remember, Nurse, that all sick leave has to be made up before the hospital can award you your certificate.'

Back on duty after the operation, life quickened its pace towards the State Preliminary examination. Already delayed by my illnesses, my lectures and classes were increased and actual 'off-duty' times dropped to a minimum. An hour's class and a meal break made a fair hole in the daily allotment of two hours off duty; and after supper there were the day's lectures to be recorded, in neat handwriting, in my study books.

The written papers were taken and the day of the practical examination arrived. With another nurse (a staunch friend then and still to this day), I set off for a large general hospital in Central London. Our shoes shone with polish and elbow-grease, stocking seams were straightened, and we carried our carefully laundered uniforms in a large brown-paper parcel.

We assumed that all the candidates, whether training in children's fever, mental or general nursing, would be taking the same examination at that stage in our careers, and it never occurred to us that our patient might be *an adult*!

Confronted by a large lady lying prone in the hospital bed, we were instructed to 'change her bed-linen completely'. We stared at each other in horror. Changing sheets to us meant lifting the child into our arms while someone else removed and then spread the clean linen in the cot. We could hardly cuddle this overweight lady; and so – in a most alarming and unorthodox fashion – we humped and bumped her around. The examiner was amazed.

This exhibition on our part was quickly terminated and our attention was turned to bandaging, then considered to be the 'party piece' of a good nurse, especially one having a knowledge of the many complicated forms. I was told to apply an eye bandage to a young lad and then … 'You can help your companion, as she doesn't seem to know which of the poor woman's breasts is to be supported.' Sister

Tutor, in passing, had mentioned the special pattern to be used after a radical amputation of breast, but as our patients had never exceeded the age of twelve years, it had not come into our practice. We wallowed in a tangled welter of wide muslin until I murmured in despair, 'We've only ever nursed children.'

Fortunately for us, the examiner had a sense of humour, and I heard her chuckling good-naturedly as she whispered an explanation to her colleague before leading us off to some lively youngsters in familiar-looking cots. Those children, bless them, were our salvation, and we both passed our examination. At a later stage in her career, that same friend became a senior nursing examiner. I do hope she was as generous to her candidates.

Back in our own domain, routine continued as before. Sister Medical made her ward rounds, then sat at her desk sedately. Remote, unperturbed by any upset, whatever the cause. Her knowledge and skills were obvious but she always seemed to me to live in another sphere to which I could never aspire. Deep as the division between sister and nurse was, I could find no bridge by which to cross. Had the patients with whom she'd had to spend her days made her like this? Or had her attitude affected them in any way? For I found the medical patients very different from those on the surgical wards.

Lustreless eyes were raised to mine, faint smiles drifted across pallid faces as I made my way around their cots. No Cockney lads jeered at my faults, no robust babies yelled and screamed for their feeds. Here, meal times took longer, for the very sickly children had to be coaxed to finish their cereals, and the babies took much persuasion to take their bottles. I missed the bustle, the drama of surgery, while the icy calmness of Sister Metcalfe made me long to be back with the dear Sister Lake.

After my stint on medical, I was moved to the tonsil ward. And that was ... an experience. Three times a week, ten children, of assorted ages and sizes, were admitted. Written instructions had been sent to the patient's parent or guardian that no food or drink was to be consumed after midnight of the day prior to admission. But, coping with soiled bed-linen, I realized that parents thought that instruction did not actually mean that the child could not have some slices of bread and jam for breakfast.

Swiftly, after I had prised the weeping or excited children from their escorts, the patients were dressed in pyjamas, bathing-type caps and rubber bibs. Everything was clearly marked with the cot number. Then, when they were seated together on a theatre trolley, a porter would wheel the trolley load of children along the corridors to the outpatients' operating theatre. When they were returned, semi-conscious, they were minus the tonsils which had been 'nipped off' with a 'guillotine' instrument.

Swathed in a long rubber apron which nearly hid my five foot of height, I awaited these children and sponged their bloodied faces before settling them down onto mackintosh-shrouded pillows. Mostly they dropped off to sleep with only a few whimpers, but sometimes they coughed and spluttered and cried out for their mothers. I knew I had to appear calm, but the spitting, coughing, half-conscious children held such terrors for me. I mentally agonized over thoughts of not being able to clear their throats, despite the swabs on the long sponge-holders standing ready in the bowls of iced water.

However, my companion in this bloody occurrence was a burly, grey-haired porter who had seen medical service in the 1914–18 war, and he helped many nurses, such as I, through this thrice-weekly trauma. With him on duty, I knew I could manage. As he carried them back to the ward, small children in his arms with head down, older ones prone on the trolley, he would weigh up the situation with a knowledge far greater than my own and say quietly, 'I'll wait for a minute or two with this one, Nurse.' And even though the surgeon himself might shout down the corridor, our friendly porter would not leave until the choking had stopped, the child roused and normal colouring had returned. He, the porter, was a tower of strength and the source of my confidence.

The rest of my day was spent mainly in soothing fretful children with raw, bleeding throats, checking their pulse rates for any change that might indicate the dreaded haemorrhage and trying to persuade them to eat a little of the jelly or ice-cream that was all we could offer them. Next day they were sent home, and the mackintoshes, caps and bibs all had to be scrubbed and made ready for the next admissions.

The outpatients and casualty departments duty came next, and this was entirely different from the ward work. Not for us the road accidents and police cases, for these went direct to the big general hospital not far away. Yet rarely a Monday morning passed without a badly scalded child's being admitted.

'I only put a bucket of hot water down for a minute and he pulled it all over himself,' the sobbing mother would cry. There was no constant hot water or automatic washers in homes then.

There were the heartbreaking, terrified children who had set themselves alight with matches or brushed against a candle or unguarded fire. Children screaming with earache and possibly candidates for a mastoid operation and a lengthy, painful stay in hospital. Daily there were babies with stunted growth and bowed legs whose chests bore the 'rosary' of rickets. They sat with parents on the hard wooden forms – which I had just polished – to hear the consultant talk of the need for fresh fruit, milk and sunshine. Even as he spoke and advised, he knew only too well that unemployment, poor housing and poverty hindered any such treatment.

Babies were brought in with the pinched grey faces that told of diarrhoea and vomiting. There were measles, mumps, whooping coughs and scarlet fevers always lurking around this department and often – so often – diphtheria. How many times, I now wonder, did I don a red-striped gown to lay a sick child, stark naked, into the hooded blanket held by the fever ambulance nurse? Many, many times.

The ambulance nurses were a law unto themselves. Tough, unpolished and yet with the courage quickly to open a choking patient's throat, slit the trachea and hold the cut wide until the fever hospital was reached.

Sometimes the semi-conscious child could not wait. Then we had to put a sandbag beneath the stretched neck and hold our breath as the surgeon made the quick incision and pushed in the silver tube; like the patient, we would breathe out in relief when the bubbling noise was heard and the cheeks slowly coloured again. Then, with sterile feathers, we inched out the thick grey membrane through the tube now securely tied in place.

Sister Outpatients was a restless, fidgety woman who, like a sheepdog, worried and urged her staff about their duties. She flirted archly with the consultants, cosseting their slightest whim, and steered the inexperienced young doctors through the trials and pitfalls of helping the sick children and giving confidence to the anxious parents.

I had hardly grown used to dealing with rows of babies in arms, crying toddlers squirming on the long wooden benches, before I was instructed to report to the operating theatre.

Sister Theatre was a petite perfectionist! One nurse only was permitted to work with her, and her meticulous skill made me feel I was a clumsy buffoon.

Yet, through working closely with those godlike men, the surgeons, all my fears of operations were completely overshadowed by the autoclave. This horror – a brand-new machine – had recently been installed at terrific cost and was one of the most modern in Britain. A fact of which we nurses were very proud. In it were sterilized all the requirements of the operating theatre and the wards. And now this most expensive equipment was under my sole care. Looking similar to a huge pressure cooker, it was housed on the second floor of the hospital in a small room near the theatre. Beside it hung a large chart giving explicit instructions as to which wheel, or which screw, to turn to ensure the right pressure and the right length of time for each working. It was perfectly clear to follow – as long as nothing else claimed my attention for the three hours this procedure was liable to take. Yet while this was going on, I had to clear the theatre, wash the instruments, scrub mackintoshes, repack drums with dressings, gowns and gloves; and finally, having washed the trolleys, washbasins and walls thoroughly, mop the floor and leave everything ready for any emergency that just might occur.

That autoclave, that monster, dominated my life for three months. Day after day I ran to and fro across the corridor, fearful that either the rubber tubing I had left boiling in the theatre would burn or the autoclave would blow up.

Twice a week, in addition to any theatre sterilizing I had to do, I also had the ward supplies to deal with. Numerous metal 'drums' awaited my attention, their perforated sides to be opened before they were stacked within the 'monster's' body and quickly closed as, hot and steamy, they were to be lifted out.

One late afternoon, as I was clearing up after a long day's work, a nurse pushed open the theatre doors.

'Something is wrong in the sterilizing room,' she panted breathlessly.

I dashed out to see hot water pouring from beneath the door. I switched off the power at the mains and then paddled in to consult the chart. It said nothing at all about flooding, nor how to deal with an irate porter telling me that water was pouring over the well of the hospital staircase. Theatre Sister was off duty and had gone out. Sister Lake – with half the surgical ward's electricity supply out of action – suggested rather acidly that I 'deal with the situation speedily'.

The hastily summoned electrician shook his head sadly. 'It's a job for the experts,' he stated and departed to telephone for help.

Later that evening two men arrived from the firm who had installed the machine. 'Teething troubles?' they enquired cheerfully before placing their thermos flasks and packets of sandwiches on a windowsill. It appeared to me that they were intending to be there all night. Certainly they were expecting to make a long job of it.

Night Sister sent me a cup of tea to encourage me as I sat in the theatre, cutting dressings and powdering gloves while my brain whirled. Would the hospital authorities expect me to pay for the damage? Out of my £20 a year? It would take me the rest of my life!

2   'Nothing goes on the floor but feet'

'Nurse? You got a minute?' The foreman had come to the theatre door.

'Was it my fault? Did I do something wrong?' I could barely gasp out the words for fear of the answer I would receive.

He was an oldish man, and I'm sure he winked as he replied, 'Let's just say it was a screw that worked loose. It happens sometimes and there's no need to cause any trouble. But ...' and he winked again, 'better be sure to keep your eye on that chart, *and* the clock, when you're working her next time.'

I know I must have seen many complicated and successful operations while I worked in the theatre, and I can recall a few of them. And yet I can remember, in every detail, that chart with its diagrams of how to control that monstrous machine, the hospital autoclave.

My three years of training ended and I passed my hospital and state examinations. I was a Registered Sick Children's Nurse. So what was I still doing at that hospital, consuming that awful food, or lack of it? I was making up my weeks of absence, my sick leave.

One morning I was in Matron's office giving her the report of a busy night's work as Sister was having a weekend off duty. As I finished and made to leave, Matron said, 'I think it would be unwise of you to take your general training straight away, Nurse. Your health needs to improve. I know you are very tired, otherwise I would think you had a stammer.'

I don't expect she ever knew why I laughed so loudly –

Desert Nurse

at the stupidity of her suggestion? Nor how much, how very much pleasure her remark gave me. But, taking her advice in the dutiful way we did in those days, I applied for the post of staff nurse in a large school and hospital for handicapped children. My duties would be confined to a babies' balcony, where infants under the age of two were nursed in the open air, winter and summer. Delightedly I was soon on my way to Haywards Heath in Sussex.

Fifteen babies were housed on a wooden balcony facing an orchard. Part of the balcony was roofed so that the cots could be moved according to weather conditions. Tall lamps with reflectors were adjusted to keep warm the babies who were snugly tucked into various types of sleeping-bags and Burberry bed-covers. Canvas screens were pulled down from the roof and fastened to the floor on wet and windy nights, the snap and flapping reminding me of summer shows at the end of seaside piers. On fine days, playpens were placed on the grass, and blankets spread for babies to roll around on, and gaze and gurgle at the moving branches of the apple trees above them. Once hardened to this open-air life, none of the babies slept indoors.

Unlike the older schoolchildren, few of our babies were physically handicapped. Mainly they were suffering from marasmus, the so-called 'wasting disease', seldom seen these days except on Oxfam appeals. They came to us as a 'last hope' after weeks in a children's hospital in the East End of London. Slowly their wizened old-men's faces and stick-like limbs turned into the smiles and the roundness of healthy childhood. Why? I have no real answer. I had nursed other small patients with equal care and devotion and yet never achieved such worthwhile and visible results. Maybe it was the clean Sussex air, and the peace and calm of their surroundings.

For me, the pace of life was much slower, and my colleagues more interesting, for, apart from the nursing staff, many of the teachers and physiotherapists were resident.

I alternated with another staff nurse to work three months on day duty and three months on nights. On day duty, Sister and I dealt with the sick babies and supervised two nurses and a nursery maid who cared for the older, more convalescent children.

We loved our babies. We cosseted and pampered them, rejoicing as any mother would at weight gains and fresh activities. Sending them home after a stay of three, six or even longer months, meant a real heartbreak for us. (Few of the parents had been able to afford the fare to visit their little ones.)

Dressed in a complete set of new 'woollies' and with a second spare outfit, they were taken back to the East End hospital by either Sister or myself. Sometimes we were rewarded by the welcoming light in the parent's eyes, yet often saddened by the sight of a weary-eyed, ill-fed woman taking back our cherished Mary or Martin. And I remember my tears when a 10-month-old Marjorie clung to me, sobbing bitterly as I put her into the grubby hands of her mother, who, eyeing the new clothes and remarking on their value, seemed already to be thinking of the pawnshop.

James often accompanied me on a London trip. He was an orphan of nearly two years. His father had died of tuberculosis before James was born, and his mother had succumbed to the same illness when her baby was just a few weeks old. He was then already fighting a losing battle with a serious lung infection, and no one knew what James's future would be. His aunt (his nearest relative) was always notified when we were bringing him back for further checks at the London hospital. She would wait for us at the hospital steps and call to the shabbily dressed children beside her: 'See ... there he is ... our little Jimmy. *And* riding in a *taxi* too.' The rosy-cheeked, happy little boy would cling tightly to my hand as we went into the hospital.

Those train journeys from Haywards Heath to London were anxious trips, with the sadness of the parting that lay ahead and the thought of the changes that poverty would bring to the well-fed child I was handing over, and more anxiety for the next little one I would be taking back with me to Sussex. A very sickly baby who would perhaps cry weakly all the return trip, so that fellow passengers would peer with concern and sometimes annoyance at the tiny face occasionally glimpsed among the lacy folds of our woollen 'travelling shawl'. There was no doubt that they were as pleased as I was to reach our destination, and clutching James's reins I would hurry out to the waiting taxi, for in those days a sick baby that could be carried did not qualify for ambulance transportation.

Night duty was different from any I had known. Except for the babies, I was alone for twelve hours. On wet nights, the canvas screens rattled and banged incessantly, and when the weather was fine, the moonlight weaved dark shadows across the grass and sometimes into the rooms. The calls of owls and pheasant sounded more eerie than the London traffic, and rabbits stopped their play at the scream of a vixen seeking her mate.

But I revelled in this quiet, secluded life. For the first time in my career I knew ahead when my off-duty weekends would occur. The village was a mile away, and the buses from there were few, but there was a common for delightful walks and, with my bicycle, many interesting places to explore.

Our community was such a happy one. We all rejoiced over every child's successful operation, discussed the choice for 'Mary' in the approaching Nativity play, and I became known for my willingness, sometimes eagerness, to care for the sick rabbits, injured birds and hedgehogs the children brought to me. And, of course, there was a tremendous change in diet. The food was just marvellous. I sat at a round table with Matron, sisters and teachers. There were always second helpings offered at every meal, and scones and jam appeared daily for tea. After stale bread and margarine, this was heaven.

There was one child we could not improve in health, and I often think of her as 'the Fairy Child'. She came as a special patient, her treatment being paid for by a generous lady. The child was born in India to the wife of a soldier and had had an undiagnosed fever when she was just one year old, since when she had made little normal progress. She seemed to live in a world of her own, never feeding herself – although she was able, nor ever fondling a toy. She would just stand and watch as I stood beside her and played with the woolly dogs and balls, tempting her to copy me. Her little hand would lie within mine but never clasp it. She would hear but never come to a call, but always she would be listening … listening. She seemed to enjoy and respond to voices and sounds that none of us could hear, and there were times when I could almost 'see' a spirit or presence to which she smiled and gurgled. I felt defeated in all my efforts to make contact with her, and I remember her still as a changeling, a 'Fairy Child'.

I might have stayed in that happy place for the rest of my nursing life except for the fact that, although I had worked months of duty as acting sister (during her illness), I was unable to be appointed in her place or to receive extra salary as I was not qualified in general nursing, then considered essential for any sister's post. General nursing of adults had never been my goal. But now it seemed I had to attempt this if I was to further my nursing career towards those envied 'strings' that hospital matrons wore.

Night duty and a delay on the railway were not a good start for a non-stammering interview at the London teaching hospital of my choice; and the severe-faced woman who greeted me did nothing to raise my confidence. My having a cousin on the medical staff may have been the reason why I was not rejected immediately. I was merely told, but with politeness, that my references would have to be rechecked, with especial enquiry regarding my earlier stammer, and had I perhaps considered taking my training in a smaller, less busy hospital?

I returned to my lonely night vigil on the balcony feeling utterly rejected, unwanted, so I was most surprised to receive a letter, some days later, telling me that I had been accepted by that hospital for another 3½ years' training.

Three months later the country vistas, the birds and hares playing in the orchard, the laughing, smiling children and those delicious and cosy meals at the friendly round table were things of the past. I was back with echoing corridors and draughty ventilators.

Clad in the blue dress of the preliminary training school, twenty young women walked in discreet files, two by two, like nuns in their cloisters. We were taken on guided tours around the nurses' home, into certain wards, operating theatres (not in use) and the outpatients department, escorted everywhere by a sister tutor who had her quarters with us in an isolated house in the hospital grounds.

Here we lived for two months at a cost of £25 pounds to pay for our board, lodging, uniform and equipment. We were taught anatomy, physiology, nursing procedures and hospital etiquette. In a well-equipped classroom we practised bedmaking and bandaging and inflicted every possible indignity on a doll who leaked from various orifices. After passing several strict examinations, seventeen of the twenty candidates were then permitted to enter the hospital wards.

I was allocated to a women's ward of thirty beds, mainly for accident and general surgery. This was a whirl of bedmaking, dusting, meals and bedpans. Of course, there were operations, deaths and admissions, but my part of these was merely to move the screens.

The large, heavy, wooden screens, hung with tightly gathered cretonne curtains, were stacked at each end of the long wards. Two had to be placed around a bed – three if extra beds were in use down the middle of the ward. A lift of Sister's eyebrows as she preceded the house surgeon along the ward was all that was needed to send one of us scurrying forward with the screens. Because we could not bump wheelchairs up and down stairs, we were allowed to use the lifts, and so my knees no longer ached at night, but instead the pains moved to my arms and shoulders.

For once in my life, my short stature was an advantage. Patients were kept bedfast for a week or ten days after surgery and were not allowed to raise themselves in bed. A junior nurse who could help lift heavy patients was a real asset, and as my first staff nurse was inclined to be dumpy like myself, we found that together we could almost 'sling' the women up their beds. But that, it seemed to me, was mostly my only asset.

One difference between wards of adults and those of sick

children lay in the twice-weekly visiting. Our babies were only viewed by their parents peering around a screen or through a peephole in the ward door. Here, on every Wednesday and Sunday afternoon, the women patients put on their make-up and their prettiest nighties and then watched impatiently as we dashed to and fro, trying to get everyone washed and the diet trolleys away before the tramp, tramp of visiting feet came nearer and nearer. During the next hour or so, while husbands and friends fidgeted at the bedsides, we hid ourselves in sluice-rooms or the kitchen, preparing diet trays or dressing-trolleys in readiness for the catching-up time when, with tears and kisses, the visitors would reluctantly leave.

Most of the patients regarded the junior nurses with sympathy. 'Better watch out. Sister's been looking in the lockers. Is it your day for tidying them?' And when reprimands came my way, they would whisper, 'Never you mind, ducks,' however much I deserved the reproof.

One of these was Mrs Kite. She was a lady of ... well, not very good repute, who – if the story was correct – had been knocked down by a car while arguing with a client. With both legs fractured and slung high on traction, she occupied the end bed in the ward, which, to my dismay, was the farthest from the sluice-room – an important factor, as she was also the victim of chronic cystitis.

'I'm sorry, dearie,' she would call to me, 'I need it again.'

Hour after hour I heaved and struggled to place her securely on the receptacle. Short and fat, with the problem plastered legs and dangling weights, she would puff and pant, 'I'm just like a stranded whale', though I doubt if she had ever been nearer to seeing one than Southend on Sea.

Dear Mrs Kite. How her bubbling laugh and common-sense cheered and guided me through those first weeks.

'Get on and tidy them drawers. That's your extra work for Monday afternoons,' or ' 'Ave you got them mackintoshes scrubbed yet? You've only got five minutes before you gotta get them teas.'

One evening, after an unusually quiet day, I walked to the sluice-room, carrying not only the customary cleaning gear of bucket and mop but the long-headed brush as well.

' 'Ere ... what's goin' on? Are ya spring cleaning ternight?'

I saw Sister, sitting as usual at her desk in the centre of the ward, look up; but she made no comment. Then, twenty minutes later, I stood with the other nurses in a line before her to hear the day's report on the patients. Calmly she read down the list of names, spoke of their condition, of forthcoming treatments, and then remarked, 'It is important to remember, nurses, that to ensure the hygiene of this ward the high dusting of windowledges and walls is done *every* evening and not just as the fancy takes you.'

Nothing was missed by Mrs Kite. 'Sorry, ducks,' she wheezed as she pushed a small bar of chocolate behind the bib of my apron, and to a spirited young nurse whose every limb ached after nine hours of pounding up and down the polished wooden floors, a twopenny bar of chocolate was really manna from heaven.

The month ended and I stood before the matron, hands clasped over my clean and starched apron (to change into it, I'd had to forgo my morning break) to hear the report of my ward sister and to learn that I had passed my trial period and could now purchase the striped dress of a first-year probationer in general nursing.

I wonder how many times during a nurse's training she is tempted to run away. Is it pride or ambition that prevents her doing so? All I do know is that the temptation is very real. I say 'she', for in pre-war days male nurses – except in mental establishments – were almost unknown. Which may of course explain the convent-like atmosphere in which we dwelt, for all nurses were compulsorily resident.

A bell rang at 6 a.m. By 6.30 we had to be standing in line, in our correct places, to answer as Sister called our names. With an audible 'Yes, Sister,' we walked past her and into chapel. We said a few prayers, repeated the collect for the day and then went to breakfast. By 6.50 we were surging along two long corridors ready to pull off our cuffs and button on the detachable short sleeves in which we worked. Promptly at seven o'clock we entered our respective wards.

Already one side would seem to be in chaos, washbowls

on lockers and the two night nurses engaged in a frantic onslaught against time in bedmaking. With scarcely a 'Good morning', we quickly joined in the fray. Washing patients from top to toe daily was then a strict part of nursing care, and as few patients remained in hospital once they had left their beds, there was an excess of blanket baths – completed at incredible speed, for until washings and beds were finished the ward maids were unable to sweep; and no one dared to hinder those dragons.

As a first year 'junior', I had to 'high-dust' the windows and ventilators, pull out the beds for sweeping and push them back again when the ward maid had passed; and, in between these tasks, to wash and polish the windowsills and locker tops. It always seemed a miracle to me that somehow all was ready for the sister's entry at 8.30.

Then, in with the drinks. 'Hot milk? Horlicks? Cocoa or cold milk?' and – the silent prayer – 'Please, please don't ask me to look in your locker for the biscuits Auntie May brought last night, for I really haven't time to stop.'

The screen that closed the ward was removed from the door at 10 a.m. and informed the world that 'nursing procedures were completed'. The ward was now open to medical staff, chaplains and the almoners. (Almoners were then a familiar part of hospital routine, for it was they who assessed the amount of payment the patient could afford for the in-hospital treatment.)

Usually first to come into the ward were the medical students. If they – mostly male – eyed us curiously, Sister regarded them with disdain. Any one of them who had not heeded the warnings to leave the beds tidy, clear dressing-trolleys and hang the charts in correct order would be told his errors in no uncertain terms, and if Sister saw him speak twice to the same nurse, he would be suspect for the rest of his time in the hospital. As for us, while juniors in a female ward, we dodged the students, for they were forever stopping us from getting on with our work by asking us to 'chaperone' the patient to be examined.

At noon the ward was closed again and we replaced our

cuffs to stand beside Sister at the large dinner trolley. Carefully she served and gave a name to each meal.

'Fish for Mrs Thomas, bed 1. See you prop her up well, Nurse. Chicken for Miss Brown, and ask her if she wishes you to cut it up for her,' and so on, all round the ward. The sweet course followed in the same manner. When the meal had been served and the medicines allocated, Sister went off to lunch, leaving us juniors to cope with a round of bedpans, tidying the beds and general clearing-up before we could go to our lunch. There was always a senior sister presiding over this meal, and neither new life nor death was supposed to prevent junior staff arriving on time. To walk in after Grace had been said was an unforgivable sin and worthy of the disapproving glance and a muttered, 'Don't let this happen again, Nurse.'

In the afternoon the wards were opened again for medical rounds until 4 p.m., when tea was followed by more washings, treatments and bedmaking. After supper at 6 p.m. the ward had to be 'settled', so that by eight o'clock some of the lights were dimmed as nurses scurried around with last-minute tidying of lockers, cleaning the sluice and bathrooms, before awaiting the call to 'report'. This was a moment in the day most enjoyed by the male wards. The men loved to see us lined up before the sister's desk in the centre of the ward. One could see them straining their ears to hear what was recited from a slate with the most intimate details of their bodily functions, and then they grimaced or winked behind Sister's back at any reprimand we might receive.

Their joy reached its height at 8.40 p.m., when the doors opened and the night staff nurse, followed by her junior, walked sedately up the ward – always on the left-hand side – to murmur with a slight nod of her head, 'Good evening, Sister,' and then proceed around the desk and back down the right-hand side of the ward, only to reappear almost immediately with sleeves rolled up, ready to take over the next twelve hours of duty.

Meanwhile the day staff had scuttled off to roll down their sleeves, put on their cuffs and repeat the drill. The junior, always at the end, with hands behind her back, would be trying to fasten the line of buttons, from wrist to elbow, and endure the men's comments of 'Left, right, left, right, keep in step now ...' that were audibly whispered as she passed the row of beds. The day was over, except for the hurried walk along the corridors to rollcall, chapel and supper.

At some time in these long days there were four hours of 'off-duty', and these were supposed to be taken in rotation, from 7 to 11 a.m., 10 to 2 p.m., 2 to 6 p.m. and 5 to 9 p.m. Lectures, however, had to be included in off-duty periods, which often sent the rota into chaos, and three stints of 7 to 11 a.m. in a row were extremely tiring. Even with breakfast at 8.30, a luxury, such hours were disastrous for any social life, which explains why boyfriends were almost unknown for junior nurses.

During each calendar month, two consecutive days off were given, and if permission was sought and given and an address supplied, 'sleeping out' was allowed. But if lectures fell on these two days, it was just hard luck. Lectures *had* to be attended. A late pass until midnight was allowed once every two weeks, providing the nurse already had an evening off duty, but being late for rollcall on any day immediately cancelled this privilege for a further two weeks, and that was a real disaster when it happened.

After nine months I was released from duty at 2 p.m. and told to report that evening for night duty on the men's surgical ward. And what a ward! On one side were twelve patients, mostly elderly, in various stages of treatment for prostate or bladder problems. On the other side lay a group of accident patients, mainly head injuries. Along the middle of the ward was an overflow of surgical cases.

The urological patients kept us very busy. Routine treatment then involved abdominal drainage prior to the removal of the prostate gland. Because of this, under most beds stood a bucket into which urine flowed through a rubber tube. At least, that was the intention; the reality was often quite different. Tubes strayed from their rightful positions, despite the skill of the staff nurse and my less experienced efforts. Restless, confused men struggled from flooded beds to drip trails across the floor, and as they had to drink vast quantities of water, the night was spent almost entirely pouring fluids into the patients only to try to retrieve it later. Was it any wonder that when, one Christmas, someone suggested that the theme for the ward decorations should be a well-known book, we received the prize for naming our effort 'The Water Babies'?

On the other side of the ward the 'head injuries' lay silent in coma or quietly moaning. Toileting, turning and feeding them was in sharp contrast to the restless mutterings of the 'urologs'. At least we had no chance of falling victim to the strange trance-like condition known as 'Night Nurse Paralysis'.

Routine work had to be fitted in somehow: cutting and packing the dressing-drums, tidying the shelves and desk drawers and, twice weekly, my pet hate, cleaning and polishing the medicine cupboard with its hoard of bottles, lotions and liniments.

Just inside each ward stood a large wooden cupboard, its doors and shelves polished to a high gloss. It reached from floor to ceiling, and no one under six foot in height could reach the top shelf. Imagine the irony of cleaning this between midnight and 3 a.m.! A trolley was spread with several thicknesses of towels to prevent the clinking of bottles. A bowl of soapy water, polishing-cloths to hand, and a chair. The act of leaping on and off the chair with a handful of bottles is no easy feat when trying so hard not to wake the patients. Some sisters tried to 'catch out' the night junior by sprinkling sugar or something sticky in the cupboard corners. The stoppers of all bottles were supposed to be removed, wiped and replaced, the shelves washed, dried and then polished, and it seemed to be such an endless job.

One night, in order to pull out the heavy storage jars full of lotions (known as Winchesters) housed on the bottom shelf, I was kneeling on the floor when Night Sister rustled in. Swiftly I stumbled to my feet in order to greet her. She stood gazing at me in horror.

'Nurse! What were you doing?' she demanded.

'My extra work for Tuesday. Cleaning the medicine cupboard, Sister,' I replied smugly. She wasn't catching *me* out!

'But you were *kneeling*, Nurse. Kneeling on the floor. Never, never let me find you like that again. In *this* hospital, nothing goes on the floor but feet!'

Feet? In that ward, mine rarely *left* the floor. In memory it remains a blur of wet beds, leaking tubes and the sight of a private patient, a very military gentleman, leaving his side-ward bed clad only in a short pyjama jacket and holding his abdominal tube well to one side as he said in very clipped tones, 'Evening, Sistah, evening. Just taking the dog for a walk.' Even among the wetness and the smell there was always some humour.

One morning I was summoned to the home sister's office and questioned about my health. Again the subject of my stammer was raised. Fortunately for me, a new department of speech therapy had just been opened, and I was informed that an appointment would be made for me to attend. Several days later I was awakened at 1 p.m. by a maid who presented me with a cold cup of tea and a note telling me to dress in uniform and be at this department at two o'clock sharp.

Scarcely awake and stammering badly, I sat before the speech therapist to hear for the very first time about treatment by relaxation. It seemed a badly timed conversation, but I was given a general outline and an invitation to visit the department regularly for advice and help. It was not until I had passed the state and hospital final examinations that the therapist told me that on her assessment of my problem at that first interview had hung the future of my continued training and that it had been the weary, bewildered look on my pallid, sleepy, 'night nurse' face that had convinced her that I should be given a 'second chance'.

Relaxation proved beneficial to me and, although no complete cure was achieved, there was a wonderful improvement.

Night duty was followed by three months 'in theatres'. To my great relief this did not entail any work with the autoclaves. This labour was undertaken by the hospital porters, who also dealt with electrical instruments and apparatus, the senior consultant being of the opinion that such matters were beyond the understanding of any female nurse.

Consultant surgeons were treated as gods, their slightest whim or fancy pandered to, their physical requirements studied in depth, whether it was the type of soap in the surgeons' room or the length of tape on their particular gown. Woe betide any nurse who offended one of the gods; no one would come to her defence. Like some clergy, they played as actors to an audience of students, nurses and, in greater or lesser degree, the patients. When the door from the surgeons' room opened, a silence spread across the theatre, and Sister's eyes would flash with annoyance if a nurse rattled a bowl or a student whispered. Flanked by house surgeon and dresser, the great man would start the ritual of 'scrubbing up' as we waited in awe for his first words to set the mood for that session's work.

'Anyone seen the new show at the Palladium?' he might ask, and a sign of relief would drift quietly round, while, 'There is a loose tape on my theatre gown, Sister,' boded ill for the next few hours.

However, these men gave their services free in twice-weekly sessions of outpatient, ward or operating care and took their turns on call for severe emergency work. From these periods of teaching and demonstrating their skill and knowledge to the medical students came the private patients who were sent to the surgeons' Harley Street consulting-rooms by former students, qualified and practising worldwide.

In the eyes of the junior nursing staff, the surgeons' skill – and it was a great skill – was dwarfed by their petty grumbling, such as, 'Why has a hospital outfit been laid out for me? I prefer my own to work in.' It was useless to point out that, after several night emergencies and routine sessions, their own gear was still at the laundry. Or a loud grumble because the small blanket, used to cover the stainless steel top of a theatre stool before the august bottom was placed upon it, was either too hot or not warm enough. Such petty little grumbles.

Once, as I struggled to lift high the leg of an anaesthetized six-foot patient, the surgeon murmured, 'Would one of you students take over from that silly girl?' Turning to Sister, he went on, 'Is there any reason at all why pigmy nurses need to work in my bloody theatre?'

Dutifully the students giggled at such a humorous remark, Sister withered me with a reprimanding look, and I scuttled away like a little cockroach.

One consultant anaesthetist was dreaded by all of us. He grunted and grumbled incessantly. Nothing pleased him unless it was an exceptionally pretty nurse. Not coming into that category, I suffered from his biting tongue until, one day, after a long, hot session, he queried, once again, whether I had changed the instruments on his trolley.

'Feel it,' I said, taking up a steel gag and dropping it firmly into his hand. Swearing horribly, he dropped the hot object onto the floor. 'Don't worry, sir,' I said smiling blithely. 'I have another one cooling for the patient.'

After that, he did not question me again in this way, and there were fewer grumbles.

At weekends, in addition to the routine cleaning, we climbed stepladders and washed and polished the tiled walls of the theatre suites. Perched high, I was giving my companions my version of the latest 'pop' song when the door opened and the assistant matron entered. She surveyed us calmly and then said, 'I came in, Nurses, to see why a ward maid was working in the theatre. I did not expect to find my nurses lowering themselves by singing when on duty. Please show a little dignity and continue your work in silence.'

However, when all the cleaning was done and the countless rubber gloves were washed, dried, turned and powdered, and drums packed ready for sterilizing, we were allowed to pull up the theatre stools and sit down. True, there was now the mending to be done – new tapes to sew on masks and gowns while we listened to Sister or Staff Nurse speaking to us about various instruments and theatre techniques, but we were still on duty and we were sitting down!

There was a different feel to a medical ward in an adult hospital, just as there had been in a children's hospital, compared to the bustle of surgery. After the tense atmosphere of the theatre I found myself enjoying the slower pace of a men's medical ward, yet I found a sadness that was part of the atmosphere. There were wives who smiled with their lips but not their eyes as they sat beside a husband they knew would never work again; and in the 1930s there was little help or money for any family without a breadwinner. Before antibiotics, bronchitis and pneumonia were not only 'the old man's friend' but took their toll of young lives too. And out on the balcony, extra red blankets shielding them from the London fogs, lay the TBs waiting for a bed in a sanatorium, looking ahead to the long months of treatment that might – but only might – lead to a cure. Yes, there was a slow sadness in the medical wards.

Orthopaedic, eye wards and the outpatients' departments came my way. Patients slung up to beams to cure their fractured legs; plaster beds and splints. Elderly cataract patients, confused and restless because both eyes were bandaged; weary folk sitting on hard wooden benches awaiting their turn for examination by a consultant surgeon or physician.

My worst memory is of the afternoons in outpatients when 'the veins' came in for dressings. Mostly the patients were charwomen whose lives had been spent scrubbing or standing at a washtub until their poor, ill-treated legs had broken into ulcers – ulcers that rarely healed and indeed became a source of pride to their owners. 'I been like this nigh on ten years, Nurse.' We bathed the fragile skin, wrapped swollen legs in sticky, treacle-like dressings covered with crepe bandages – which had to be washed for further use, of course – and then sent the patients off home, knowing that in a week or two the whole sickening, reeking procedure would have to be done again.

Release from this came when, owing to an outbreak of

influenza – and the advantage of my children's training, I took charge of the nursery in the maternity ward at night. It was lovely to be back among the tiny babes. Thirty or more lay in small cots, parked on double-tiered trolleys ready to be wheeled into the mothers' ward in the daytime. I spent the nights changing, bathing and feeding, sitting before a row of baby baths and trolleys that stood in the centre of the nursery. And not even their hungry chorus in the very early hours disturbed me.

Sometimes a medical student would join me during these night hours as he waited for a call from the labour ward. One eager redheaded lad often tried, under my instruction, to bath some of my young charges. After his first delivery 'on the district',* he dashed in to tell me he had '... cut the cord and bathed the baby before the midwife had arrived; and because he was rather a small little chap, and I remembered how you oiled the prems, I did him with oil after the bathing, before I put on some powder.' The student was so proud of his efforts, and I congratulated him but couldn't help wondering what sort of sticky babe the midwife found when she arrived.

One night, with several babies being born at the same time, I was pressed into helping in the labour ward and saw my first birth. I'd not expected such an event to stun me as it did, and for the rest of that duty I stared at those babies, pondering over the miracle of birth.

At Christmastime the hospital was transformed. Wards were decorated and extra visiting was allowed. Preparations began in early December with a collecting-box at the ward door requesting donations to help with the trimmings and tinsel and other decorative materials. Students and night nurses conspired over the theme and

* This phrase relates to the delivery and nursing of mothers and babies in their homes. Medical students undertake these tasks during their term of obstetrics and are helped by the district midwife (community nurse or midwife in modern parlance). Nurses complete a separate training for midwifery and become qualified practitioners in their own right, able to deliver and nurse mother and child without medical aid if all is normal.

the making of lampshades and garlands. Sisters and staff nurses thought up elaborate flower arrangements.

On Christmas Eve many of the nurses rose at 4 a.m. and set off for Covent Garden Market. Amid the bustle of the flower-filled building, uniformed nurses from most of the London hospitals moved around, marvelling at orchids from far-away lands and early daffodils from Cornwall as they added and subtracted the money available for their purchases.

'Which 'orspital you gels from then?' the traders asked. 'Oh, our Millie was in there when that bus knocked 'er darn. Give 'em another couple o' bunches, Bill. No … no extra charge.'

We hurried back, our arms laden with much that had been given freely and lovingly; and the scent of those blossoms, the resinous smell of the mounds of Christmas trees, comes back to me through the years.

No one took 'off-duty' during the Christmas period. Christmas was for the patients and their visitors, and I believe we all did our best to make it so. During the day, the wards were decorated, the male students climbing on ladders to hang the garlands and fix the lampshades while most of the women patients flirted and joked with them, or the men offered advice and criticism.

The wards were settled early on Christmas Eve, for as soon as the night staff had taken over, the carols began. All the hospital staff joined in the long procession which wound its way along the darkened corridors to stop outside each ward doorway and sing the traditional hymns. Night Sister stood by the entrance to the nurses' home to watch her demurely cloaked nurses detach themselves from the white-coated throng of students and housemen before she thankfully locked the door. Those who had slipped away had already planned their return by fire escape or unlatched window at some later time.

On Christmas morning all but the very sick patients managed an extra smile or a cheery greeting as we spruced them up for daylong visiting. Santa Claus, the hospital committee, doctors, students, nurses and ward maids toured the ward to gossip with patients and admire the decorations. No one was allowed to feel lonely or unvisited on this day. The sick ones, the dying, were taken to a side ward, if they could be moved, to ensure a little privacy as we prayed that death would not come and dampen the festive spirit we were trying so hard to produce; and I remember too how the grieving relatives tried hard to keep their sadness and anxieties from the other patients.

At midday the ward would be crowded as, dressed as a chef, the senior consultant would stride in, brandishing a huge knife with which to carve the turkey. In a surgical ward, his entry was always received with a cheer. Except in very severe cases, all dietary rules were relaxed and generous helpings of traditional fare were served to everyone. As for us, we slipped away in turn to the nurses' dining-room, where cold meat, sliced beetroot, cold custard and stewed fruit awaited us. The patients' visitors came for the afternoon, and by the time the night staff came on duty the lights were dimmed and most of their charges were, like ourselves, exhausted and ready for sleep.

The coloured lampshades over the beds, shadowy in the feint light from the centre shade, the gifts of flowers now a bank of colour in the corridor and the fragrance of the Christmas tree are special memories I hold, seeing them as an oasis in a desert of familiar routine.

Boxing Day was different again. The hospital provided tea to all the patients' visitors after we'd spent the morning in the ward kitchen buttering scones, making sandwiches and slicing cake. In the evening everyone capable of being moved was wheeled or pushed in their beds to watch the students' 'Christmas Show'. This was a musical performance, put on for two nights, to the great delight of patients and nurses. Somehow every year there was always someone in the medical school with a flair for music, a talent for libretto, and on many occasions the show was good enough to have graced a London stage. Written and rehearsed in sparse off-duty time and costumed by women whose fingers were more used to surgical needles, these yearly musicals were a source of joy and relaxation to audience and actors alike.

I was tired. Desperately tired. My exams lay behind me,

although the results were still awaited, and the ward to which I was now sent was dreaded by all nurses. The sister had a reputation for perfection and demanded this at all times on her female medical ward. I had not worked there previously, and now I found myself her second-in-command, the senior staff nurse. From the first day I felt her eyes following me wherever I walked. I tried, really hard, to meet her ideals and follow her techniques, but my efforts never seemed to please. There were always the same questions, how and why, what and where?

'Only a few more weeks,' I consoled myself, and then came Sister's long weekend off, which was a rare privilege. From lunchtime on Friday until Monday afternoon, the ward was in my care.

Early on Saturday morning a patient suffering from pneumonia had to be put into an oxygen tent – then, a time-consuming, complicated affair. By lunchtime a very ill girl had been diagnosed as a typhoid fever case. For reasons unknown to me, these patients did not go to the isolation hospitals but were nursed in their original wards under strict 'barrier care'.

I had been taught the special procedures, but had never seen them in use, for this disease. First, a detailed list had to be sent to the stores requesting any item of red crockery, hardware etc. that could possibly be needed. As it was a Saturday, the stores were closed, and this required much tracking down of the storeman on call. I read the list through and through again, thinking of everything from an egg-cup to the bright red covers for the screens that shielded the patients. The wardmaid had to be recalled to duty to scrub away the polish and thus mark out the prescribed areas around the bed. I reorganized the sluice room to provide separate space for bins and specimens. I was late going off duty that night.

On Sunday two cardiac patients were admitted. One of them in severe distress, and between 7 a.m. and 9 p.m. I managed to get only one half-hour lunch break.

When Sister returned, she did a complete round of every patient. I followed behind, answering her questions. Then we retreated to the linen room, where, seated at either side of the table, we pored over charts, prescriptions and pathological reports. By the second tea time, when I was due to go off duty, I could barely keep my eyes open. At least, if there had been no praise and no sympathy for such a busy time, there had been no adverse comments, no pointing out of omissions in the records of treatments and drugs. I was just putting on my cuffs, preparing to murmur a weary 'Goodnight, Sister,' when the keen dark eyes looked up at me as Sister put down her pen to ask, 'When you ordered the special red crockery, you did not ask for any flower vases. Surely you should have thought of them?'

Next morning I asked leave to go to the office with a special request. I wished to ask for a transfer to another ward. Sister stared at me in amazement before she asked my reasons. I blurted out that I did not wish to remain where I was considered incompetent. There was a pause before, slowly, as if explaining to a young child, Sister informed me that she did not waste her time on poor material, that she had judged my nursing to be of a high standard and, because of that, she had devoted considerable time and effort in trying to polish whatever talent I possessed. There was no need to discuss the matter further.

Perhaps she realized she had pushed me too hard, perhaps my general fatigue showed, but after that conversation I was left to work without supervision.

A very sick girl was admitted as a rheumatic fever case, and she died after a few hours with us, but not before she had spread some virulent form of throat infection to several nurses. We worked shorthanded for several weeks until one morning I asked Sister, 'Do adults suffer from erythema nodosum? I have only seen it in children.'

'Yes, but it is unusual. Why do you ask?'

We went into the linen room, and I showed her the lumps and bruises on my legs.

'A good diagnosis,' was her only comment as she moved forward to reach a chair in which to wheel me to the sick room.

Those with sore throats had days off duty; I had many

weeks and then a spell of convalescence at home. But there was no escape: even though my examination results were good, I had to return and make up the time lost through sickness.

As a State Registered Nurse, now on two registers, I was sent to night duty in casualty department. It was not every person's choice, for, except for an elderly porter tucked away in a cubbyhole by the entrance doors, I was alone for many hours, the empty hall echoing to the clink of metal as I cleared and prepared trolleys, cut and packed dressings. At 10 p.m. the students – called casualty dressers – went off duty unless we were very busy; and at 11 p.m. the medical officer went to his quarters to be called as and when required. He had been a house surgeon while I had been working on a surgical ward, so after a few nights 'to let me find my feet' he often left the minor sutures and suchlike to me, quite unknown to Night Sister, of course.

I enjoyed my work there, partly, I think, because there was so much variety. One never knew what the night would bring. Sometimes the hall would be full when I went on duty, fractured arms and legs being plastered, cut heads to be stitched after a pub brawl, a very sick patient to be rushed to a bed in a ward. It might be midnight before the benches were emptied, the cubicles vacant, and I had very little time to fit in the routine work of checking supplies and drugs. There was a two-bedded ward to be supervised, usually occupied by patients who had taken a general anaesthetic badly or had a heavy plaster that needed to dry.

In the early hours of the morning men from the local printers might call in with a boil to be dressed, a finger cut or bruised by a machine, and they always brought me a newspaper, wet from the presses. On cold, wet nights, whatever the hour, there were 'the regulars', tramps who managed to fall down just as a policeman was passing on his beat. A fit? A slight stroke? Who could say? They always gave an address outside our 'free area', but of course they never had any money to pay for ambulance extra mileage. So they slept the night in the warmth of a casualty cubicle. The porter usually managed to scrounge them some breakfast, and then he and I would be occupied with our respective duties. A few minutes later the outside door slammed, and only the empty dishes remained to tell of an overnight resident. I would bundle the red blankets into the sack for disinfecting and wonder which hospital they would honour with their presence on the next night of bad weather, for they seldom turned up too frequently at the same place.

The police often brought drunks and badly bruised people – perhaps after a street fight – but in the three months I was on duty I saw only one stab wound and two of gunshot. So different from the nights in casualty these days.

The warning of an ambulance bell sounding after midnight sent me running outside, midwifery bag in hand, for it was either a baby already or about to be born or a DOA (Dead On Arrival). If it was the latter, the ambulance men would often keep me away. 'A messy suicide,' they'd say and wait until the medical officer had been called.

One night they brought in an elderly woman, dirty and smelly, whom the police had found beside a flight of riverside steps. Uncertain whether or not she was dead, they carried her in. As I moved her ready for the doctor's inspection, I found her petticoat was weighed down with coins and notes; there were some hundreds of pounds stitched into pockets all round the hem. Her thin, half-starved daughter, called in by the police, sobbed pitifully as she explained how, with difficulty, she and her husband had tried to help 'Mum', who had only her small pension. She bit her lips in dismay and confided that she had no idea how they would pay for the funeral but hated the idea of Mum's having a pauper's burial, as Mum never had enough to pay any insurance. Casualty was most certainly a big eye-opener for me.

3 *Out and about*

The matrons of the teaching hospitals, in the late thirties, were told to ask suitable, trained nurses to put their names forward for the reserve branches of the armed services, to be called on in the event of a national emergency.

A request, in those times, was virtually a command. I completed and sent in my form to the Queen Alexandria Imperial Military Nursing Service, and after a brief interview at the War Office I was accepted with the rank of sister. All nurses, QAs as they were known, had then to be on two or more of the nursing registers, so sister was the lowest rank in the Corps. No duties were called for, but I was sent a heavily sealed packet, to be opened 'Only in the event of WAR'. In my blissful ignorance, I smiled as I dismissed such rumours of war as hypothetical invention. This was 1938.

I had other, more important things on my mind. What to do next? I felt strongly that no training was complete without a midwifery certificate, and when some unexpected money came to me from a relative, my mind was made up. I would take the short midwifery course, for which, by paying fees and laundry, the specialized training could be taken in six months instead of having to work at the maternity hospital for a year after qualifying, in order to repay the fees. The big London hospitals were much too expensive to be covered by my small windfall, so I applied to a Sussex hospital and was accepted for training to commence at a later date.

To bridge the gap and to build up my finances, I was fortunate enough to get on the staff of London's best-known nursing agency, run by Noel Coward's aunt.

In the nurses' hostel I awaited my first call. This was to a child with measles, a most profitable call, as a week's quarantine period had to be paid to me. It also happened to be a 'measles year', and the agency sent me out again within hours of my return, and then followed a succession of cases. Mostly they were in the Home Counties, and one was at a boarding school where I did night duty to help the overworked school matron and her staff.

My savings mounted. My train fares, laundry and expenses for the next six months were assured and safe. It had been so easy to save on my £7 a week.

And then I was informed: the midwifery course was about to begin.

I soon found myself being greeted by another matron: 'I'm glad you came early. I've assigned you to night duty. You will report at 8 p.m.'

Night Sister was a large-bosomed woman who, when not supervising in the labour ward, liked to kick off her shoes, unbuckle her belt and doze comfortably in the office chair. Hearing of my children's certificate, she directed me to the nursery with, 'I don't want to hear the babies bawling all night.' To my amusement, she confided to one of my colleagues later that week that, with me in the nursery, there were no troubles at all. Had she bothered to come around in the wee small hours, she would have found all the noisy babies pushed close to the radiators in the bathrooms, well out of earshot.

Her accent and demeanour would not have suited my London teaching hospital standards. She ranted at the labouring women, urging them to 'Push ... push ... get on with the bloody job you've got to do.' Then just at the moment of birth her mood would change, and a drawling, affected voice would say, 'There, there, mothah. Your little bebe will soon be hear-ah.' However, she guided me through my first fumbling deliveries with skilful concern, until I was changed to day duty.

From the first, Day Sister and I did not take to each other. She disliked premature infants and accused me – probably correctly – of spending too much time with them and neglecting my other work. And she disliked intensely anyone who stammered. Her attitude only made me worse.

'I don't know why I should be tormented like this,' Sister flung at me one day. 'The consultant surgeon stammers, last year the house surgeon was as bad, and now I have you to put up with. It is nothing but a habit. And a bad habit. And I will not put up with it in front of my mothers.'

'I came here to learn midwifery,' I retorted angrily. 'That was what I paid my fees for. Not to be insulted.'

Later, with head held high – to increase my height as I do when I am annoyed – I faced the assistant matron.

'I'm quite sure no insult was really intended. Sister has been unwell and she has to work very hard, you know.' The words were spoken in a calming tone. 'Now please go back to your ward, and I will have a word with Sister.'

I have no idea of the conversation that took place between Matron and Sister, but from that day onwards any words between us were very sparse, and all my work was supervised by the junior sister. I had no regrets when I left the hospital to do three months 'on the district'.

There were six pupils in the roomy old house on the edge of a cluster of smaller houses. The narrow streets ascended steep hills leading from the beaches and the more affluent side of town. We walked or cycled to and from our patients; our deliveries were watched by one of three midwives; then, as trained nurses, we were left to nurse the mothers and babies on our own.

The patients paid fees to the hospital for our services for a period of fourteen days after the birth. They were charged £1. 10s. for the first child, and £1 only thereafter. This included all ante-natal care and the services of the hospital's doctors if required. There were few complaints about this fee, even though a working-man's wage barely reached £3. Each patient was given a list of bed-linen and utensils that were required for the delivery, including coppers for the gas meter or for emergency telephone calls. And, of course, a pile of newspapers with which to protect the floor and mattress; plastic sheeting was unknown.

It was strange, yet comforting, that from the moment we leaned the bicycle against the house fence we became members of the family. Whether neat and tidy or rough and ready, the house and its occupiers showed a welcome that was quite sincere. The anxiety and expectation of the relatives waiting for the birth were expected to be shared by the nurse, but in the nicest, friendliest way. We were all there to welcome the newcomer to the family circle. This was all so different from the regimented order of hospital routine. Here there was the time to admire the – often handsewn – baby gowns as they were placed on the clothes-horse waiting beside the bedroom fire; time to discuss the new wallpaper, especially hung for this great event, and time to discourage the fleas and bedbugs with which the area abounded. The mother was calm too, knowing, as she walked around the familiar bed or leant against a worn chair, that no matter how long it took, if everything was normal, there'd be no change of staff, no stranger taking over just when her need was greatest.

Quite soon I learned when to send the husband back for the supervising midwife so that she did not get annoyed with me for getting her out of bed too soon. I knew which house had a saucepan large enough to boil up the forceps should they be required, and I could spot the embroidered traycloth borrowed from someone in the next street for the 'after-delivery tea'. This was a ritual that no one would forgo. When mother and baby had been tidied up and when the anxious father had beamed his way into the bedroom from which he had been totally excluded, it was Grandma's – or an elderly neighbour's – hour of triumph. Carefully she would carry in a tray of tea, and on the lace-edged or embroidered traycloth sparkled the best china (often the same china that I had drunk from at a previous local birth), a large china teapot and a plate of biscuits. Sometimes even a cake! This was our celebration. Our joy in the wonder of womanhood.

Moving around the streets at night held no terrors for us nurses. The senior midwife advised us to leave the lower buttons of our uniform coats undone so that the stiff white aprons clearly showed. 'No one will touch you,' she maintained. 'Everyone respects a nurse on duty.' And she was right. I never knew anyone in the nursing profession who ever felt any nervousness when walking or cycling after dark. The policemen on the beat were our special friends. Often, as I wheeled my bike up a steep hill, one of them would enquire, 'Are you going to number 46? It's just around the corner. All the lights are on to show you they are waiting for you.'

One early dawn, when I was making my way to the nurses' home after I'd had a long spell with a first baby, suddenly a policeman shouted from across the street, 'Come here, quick!' He grabbed my arm and hurried me towards an open doorway. 'First floor front,' he directed, and a woman on the doorstep sobbed.

I followed the policeman up the steep stairs to see a woman on a double bed, sprawling on top of a bright yellow satin eiderdown. From her grunts and groans, birth seemed imminent. The policeman held her legs as she thrashed around, and within minutes there was a tiny but living baby.

'Cor!' sighed the policeman. 'She smells worse than a brewery.'

I realized then that the woman was very drunk.

At the sound of the baby's cries, the woman downstairs who had sobbed made her way in to tell us that the mother was a 'weekend bed-and-breakfast' guest. The man she'd come in with had made a quick getaway and was not seen again. Several days later the woman disappeared, leaving behind her not only her unpaid bill but her baby also. The yellow satin eiderdown had to be destroyed.

Then, of course, I was in disgrace. I had nursed a patient who had not paid any fees, and I had taken dressings and baby clothes from the 'charity box'; most certainly I could not be allowed to include her in my examination folio because I had dared to make a delivery without a senior midwife being present to witness the procedure. Good deeds do not always bring rewards, I discovered.

The work 'on district' interested and satisfied me. I made up my mind that this was where my future lay, and I applied to become a member of the Queen's Institute of District Nursing.

Suddenly my plans had to be changed. My uncle, much loved by me and with whom most of my childhood had been spent, became ill with cancer. If he survived the pain-relieving surgery, he would need skilled nursing for the rest of his life. I knew where my duty lay. I cancelled my application and arranged to take on his care as soon as I was free.

But while I was taking my final midwifery examinations, he quietly passed away.

The letter that came from Dorothy, one of my friends in my general training, held a twofold message. She sent her sympathy on my uncle's death and a suggestion that, as I had cancelled my district work, I should join her in Cornwall for a few weeks.

Dorothy was purchasing a large house to convert into a nursing home. 'There is only one decent one in the entire West Country,' she wrote, with exaggeration, 'so there is plenty of scope, and I should be glad of your help in equipping the home when the builders have moved out. Meanwhile, if you wish to make a little money, I have also acquired a nurses' agency. Do come. Cornwall deserves some decent, up-to-date nursing. They are still in the Nightingale era here.'

The sheer beauty of Falmouth delighted me, and Dorothy's mother made me feel most welcome, even in a house in which builders were creating havoc.

I soon took up Dorothy's offer and set out for my first patient, having her second baby in an isolated farmhouse. An elderly maid led me up the stairs to my bedroom, left me with my suitcase and was conveniently dusting the stair banisters as I came out of the room to find my way down to my patient. She eyed me, or rather my uniform, from top to toe as I stood before her on the stairs.

'Ho! So you're not a proper nurse, then?' she queried, hoisting herself upright so that I could pass her.

'Of course, I am,' I said with a little chuckle. 'But why do you think that?'

'Proper nurses here wear white handkerchief veils on their head and proper aprons with straps to them.'

Black straw bonnets and long cloaks too, no doubt, I thought. So much for my modern and expensive outfit, fresh from Robinson & Cleaver's Regent Street store. I wore a small American-style cap of spotted muslin, lace-trimmed, a square-bibbed apron fastened to my royal blue dress with a neat gold pin and my hospital badge. Oh, well!

Oil lamps and Elsan toilets had never come my way before. Neither had family rows. The baby and his elder brother were pleasant children, but the parents! They were young, both from old-established Cornish families, rich in legend but short of cash. The wife had been reared in the town and found it very hard to accept the problems of farming. No doubt it was not easy to hear the milk machine churning away outside while she had to struggle with oil lamps and flat-irons in the house. I felt sorry, too, for the young husband, when his gift of chocolates followed him through the bedroom door onto the staircase, where the farm dogs gobbled them up.

I was glad when the time came for me to return to the noisy and chaotic clatter of the builders and to some routine of daily visits to hotel guests requiring injections, dressings or baths. I soon became known to the hall porters of these big establishments, many of which kept open in the winter for elderly residents who spent the summer months with relatives or in small cottages until the autumn chills sent them back to the hotels.

Sometimes I would leave the piles of sheets and towels we were marking in the home to answer an emergency call when a baby arrived early and the 'monthly nurse' was booked to attend another case. Or when a doctor asked for a well-trained nurse for an influential patient. Which was how I came to stay in a large country mansion.

The owner was an elderly lady who suffered from recurrent attacks of a painful condition requiring complete rest in bed. She was very aristocratic but pleasant and considerate, and I found the house interesting, while the grounds were a source of wonder to me. Each afternoon I wandered among flowering camellias and rare shrubs, unless the gardener had been requested to take me up-river in an ancient launch.

Every morning after breakfast the entire staff of servants gathered in the dining-room. Chairs were brought in to the far end of the room, wooden benches were placed behind them, and three armchairs were then placed in the front for the housekeeper, butler and cook. In the back row sat the gardeners and the chauffeur. My patient's cousin – her constant companion – read a short lesson and prayers from a lectern at the other end of the room. My chair, upholstered, was placed midway. I decided I must be neither fish nor flesh nor good red herring.

My patient slowly improved and spent much time questioning me about my home, my education and my training. She found my idea of becoming a district nurse most surprising.

'My dear girl, you must not waste all those years at school and hospital by going around cottages. Our district nurses here manage quite well with only a couple of years' study at the local sanatorium. I know this is a fact because I am chairman of the committee.'

Her knowledge made me conceal a smile ...

While I was there, a distant member of the family died in London, and the cousin travelled to attend the funeral. This meant that for several days I lunched and dined alone in the huge dining-room. Alone, that is, except for a butler and footman in attendance for my requirements. I did not enjoy the experience. In fact, it was a nightmare eating unfamiliar food presented to me on silver salvers, and in my youthful embarrassment I refused several dishes which I longed to try if only I had known how to deal with them. I was glad when the cousin returned, and a few days later I went back to the home, where our first baby was due to arrive.

Sometimes I was very busy, as Dorothy had not taken her midwifery training and I was therefore required to be at hand whenever any maternity patients had been admitted. But further extensions were planned, so I was able to take patients in other parts of the country. I seemed to have an attraction towards vicarages ...

The first was a stone building around a square courtyard with outside staircases connecting the two floors. The house was entered by a small bridge over a stretch of water on which dwelled a noisy family of ducks.

'Don't worry if you meet a ghost here,' the vicar said lightly as he led me towards his wife's bedroom. She was resting following a leg injury. 'We often see her around this passage. Part of this house was built in the fourteenth century, and that's where we think she belongs. I just say a prayer for her as we pass but she never does anyone any harm.'

My prayers would be for myself, I thought, as I followed him, but the ghost never appeared to me. However, an old spaniel gave me a terrible fright one evening when, called by my patient, I pattered along the passage in my dressing-gown and slippers and the dog stole up behind me to lick my bare legs.

Going out for a walk here had its problems too, as the front drive was guarded by a flock of Chinese geese who seemed to take a strong dislike to me. Perhaps I did not have the right technique in threatening them with a stout walking-stick. A pile of these were kept at the house and gate for this very purpose. The path that led to the church held equal terrors, for a herd of lively bullocks cavorted towards me whenever I walked there. Maybe it was one way of keeping too many parishioners from calling with minor requests.

Once again I ate in a huge dining-room where, after the maid had struggled up the outside stairs with a tray of covered dishes and left us alone, the vicar and I had to rise from our chairs and walk if we wished to pass any plate or dish to each other. Tea was served to me alone in the drawing-room. Dainty plates of bread and butter, small cakes and one large plain or iced cake. Being well brought up, as I thought, I did not cut the big cake until the fourth day of my stay, after the cook had accosted me to say acidly, 'Would you please cut the big cake today, Sister? I'm not allowed to use any cake in the kitchen until it has been cut upstairs, and if *you* don't like my fruitcake, the staff do.' After that, whether I wanted any or not, I solemnly cut the big cake each afternoon.

Then I went to a town rectory where most of the children and their mother were suffering from whooping cough. Apart from the invalids, I found myself dealing with the telephone, helping out in the kitchen, where staff was minimal, and even losing myself in unfamiliar streets as I tried to locate the rector with urgent messages from sick or anxious parishioners. Money was tight in that house, and my busy, yet enjoyable stay lasted only a few days.

It was only the urgent pleading of the doctor, who was well known to us, that made Dorothy ask me to turn out one very stormy night.

'The patient is a very sick old clergyman who's had a severe stroke, and Doctor doesn't think he will last the night, but his housekeeper is worn out with nursing. It will only be for tonight. You can come back in the morning, and if he's still with us, we will arrange for someone else to carry on.'

She took me into Helston (any cross-country journey in Cornwall seemed to go through Helston), and I managed to catch the last bus to a small village. There were only a few people aboard but it seemed to me that every head turned as I asked the conductor to put me down at the nearest point to the vicarage. It was because of my London accent, I presumed, until an elderly woman sitting opposite leaned forward to touch my knee.

'We heard as how the poor man was very ill. Are you family?'

'No,' I told her. 'I'm going to nurse him tonight.'

'Nurse him, Miss?' She stared in amazement. 'Oh, they shouldn't be sending a little maid like you! Not to *that* house!'

I smiled at her. I was quite used to it by now, the Cornish habit of calling any unmarried young woman a 'little maid'.

The bus stopped and the conductor beckoned me. The road was unlit and the rain pouring down as I pushed open the rickety iron gates.

'Be you Nurse?' An old man crouching under a bush for

shelter startled me. Candle in jamjar, spluttering in the rain, he led me by its dim light along a driveway where the trees offered no shelter, only drips onto my face and neck. Then the kitchen door opened. The room's light and warmth seeming normal and comforting.

An elderly woman, the housekeeper, I presumed, fussed over me, shaking my wet coat and pouring me some hot tea before – lamp in hand – she led me upstairs and into a small dressing-room.

'Master is through here,' she nodded, indicating a door standing ajar. 'I thought you could change your things here and then read the note the doctor has left you. There's little to do for the poor man, and I will bring you up a tray with a flask and some sandwiches before I go to bed.'

There *was* little for me to do, according to the doctor's letter: 'Don't ring me between midnight and seven, unless you think there is any way that I can help.'

I took off my coat, put on my apron and went into the dimly lit bedroom. The man who lay in the large bed looked as if he had already left this world, his shallow breathing scarcely moving the sheet across his chest. He reminded me of a stone-carved figure in a church tomb.

I turned suddenly as I heard a snore coming from nearby. Huddled deep in an armchair was a very elderly woman. Poor soul, I thought. His wife, I supposed, worn out by worry and nursing. Perhaps later I could persuade her to go to bed. Then the door burst open and another woman, in a bright, gaudy dress, erupted into the room.

'Look at all these medicines! I don't like medicines!' She swung out her arm towards some bottles on the mantelpiece.

'Shush!' I tried to quieten her, realizing that, despite her bright dress, she was, in fact, a middle-aged woman.

'Time you were in bed,' came a strong voice from the doorway, and I watched with relief as yet another woman appeared and took the noisy one by the arm. She nodded a greeting to me, murmured, 'I'll be back,' and they both went from the room.

'Sorry about that,' she said on her return. 'I am the elder

daughter. As no doubt you saw, my sister is not quite normal. She has gone to bed now and won't trouble you again.

'Is there no change?' she asked, glancing towards the still figure in the bed. Her hard face softened. 'The doctor has told us ... But when ... if anything happens during the night, don't call me. I'm useless at nursing, or deathbed scenes. You are very young. Will you be all right here, alone?' She brushed her hair back from her face wearily. 'This has happened at a bad time. I've been working hard. I have an exhibition soon.'

I realized then that she was wearing a very stained smock. Was she a painter? Sculptress? Cornwall was full of them.

'I shall be all right,' I told her. 'You can sleep, for I shall not leave your father alone. But should I waken your mother if I see any change for the worse?' I indicated the armchair.

'My mother? Oh, I didn't notice she was there. Would you be good enough to help me get her to her room?'

The drunken women I had met in casualty departments had often brightened a quiet night with their restless shouting, striking out at the policemen who had brought them in for a cut head to be stitched or a bruised eye to be examined. This shuffling, stumbling woman was different but the smell of her breath was exactly the same. Together we steered her into a nearby bedroom, laid her on the bed and covered her with a blanket.

The night hours were long, the creaking noises in that damp old house unexpected and eerie. I kept the lamp turned high and the coal fire blazing until, just before daylight came, the old man's breathing faltered and in a minute his life had ended. There was no night sister, no colleague, to kneel beside me as in years gone by, to say the prayers that had been part of our hospital routine. But I said them just the same for this frail old clergyman whose life had ceased. I was glad when I had carried out, 'this, my last act of love'.

I had packed my case by the time the housekeeper looked in.

'When?' was all she asked as she pulled aside the sheet and murmured, 'He was a good man.' Then, in her practical way, she hurried off to light the fire and make me some breakfast.

The doctor came after my telephone call and offered to take me back to the village to catch an early bus. Outside, the sun shone warm and bright, the leaves of the trees green and shining after last night's rain. I was glad to leave behind me that house of sadness where the wallpaper ballooned in damp corners and the threadbare curtains waved like tattered battle flags at unwashed windows.

Years later I used that setting for a short story. Rejecting it, the editor said, 'What made you place the story in a vicarage? It made it seem even more impossible.'

The builders finally finished, and most of my work was now centred on the home. To help with the running-costs until it became well known, Dorothy took three permanent patients, a doctor and his disabled wife, and an elderly lady. Geriatric patients were seldom nursed in the voluntary hospitals in which I had trained, and long-stay patients were moved to other establishments, so it came as a great surprise to me that they became favourites of mine, and I looked forward to my routine duties with them. The doctor told me of years spent overseas, and the widowed lady was a fund of information about Cornwall, where she had spent all her days. I called into her room one night to tell her of the safe arrival of our latest baby.

'He has red-gold hair,' I told her.

'Oh, please, do let me see him,' she pleaded. 'I have never seen a newborn babe with red hair.'

'He didn't have a very easy entry into the world,' I told her, 'and you look tired. You both need rest. I'll let you have a peep when I bath him in the morning.'

She had another heart attack and died that night. I shall always wish I had let her glimpse her first redhead.

One of my patients lived on a remote farm, reached more easily by the ferry than by road. They were anxious parents who had waited long for their firstborn, and I was a welcome visitor on my half-days off. Frequently on these ferry trips I met a man whose work took him that way. We became friendly but not quite friendly enough to make me give up my idea of getting my certificate in district nursing. Perhaps, when I had that, I would come back to Cornwall? At the moment I could not feel certain ...

4   *Desert song – and dance*

It was not to be, that district nurse's training. At the end of August 1939 I found myself at the gates of Netley Military Hospital.

'You'll be needing the Voluntary Aid Detachment quarters, Miss,' the large sergeant dealing with the press of men around him said, looking down at me disparagingly, 'not the sisters' block. We'll be needing plenty of you girls to help with the hospital work and cooking. There's a sign along there that says VAD nurses' quarters.'

I shook my head and learnt my first lesson in the Army – always have your orders to hand. He glanced at them after I had fumbled in my bag, and then shouted to a passing soldier, 'Take the sister's baggage up! You follow him, Ma'am.' No one had ever called me that before.

The sister who welcomed me – though those are hardly the right words – exclaimed, 'Another one? I have no idea what I'm supposed to do with all you ... er ... people. Anyhow, you are lucky, you can have the last bedroom. Have you brought bed-linen and towels?' She tut-tutted at my negative reply as she ushered me into a large room with an unmade bed. 'Well, I'll have some linen sent up later. Meanwhile just get out your napkin and ring and come with me, otherwise we shall be late for dinner.'

As I followed her upright figure, immaculate in grey dress, scarlet cape and flowing cap, I felt depressed. It was obvious I should be no good if hostilities did commence, for I had not had the sense to include a table-napkin and ring in my preparations for war.

It was on 3 September that I heard the declaration of war – whilst seated on the floor in the crowded sisters' mess. No one spoke as we made our way back to our bedrooms, seeking a few moments of quietness to let the news sink into our minds. It was the last quiet time I can remember in that hospital, which seemed to explode with loud voices, trampling feet and the incessant ringing of telephone bells.

All the talk seemed to be of 'units'. The one to which I had been assigned – a large field hospital, whatever that might mean – seemed to require the nursing staff to assemble frequently to meet the matron, only to have to repeat the interview in a few hours' time when another matron was appointed.

We were given passes to travel to London and to buy our uniforms at Harrods in Knightsbridge, a delightful store in which previously 'window shopping' had been the nearest I had ever achieved. This indeed was a Red Letter Day. By the time I had bought my topcoat and mess dress, however, the uniform allowance of £20 was almost spent, and I had to dip into my savings to complete the list of grey cotton dresses, aprons, caps, belts and cape, all to be sent back to the hospital.

I then went on to another department, in which harassed men spread unfamiliar objects before me and advised me on the purchase of my camp bed, folding chair, canvas bath, basin and bucket, blankets, travelling-rug, pillow, towels and *green-lined white parasol*!

Along to the ironmongery department for a hurricane lamp, cutlery, plates ... I couldn't believe I would need so much. Then, of course, I had to purchase a large tin trunk and several valises to accommodate this colossal mound of clothes and equipment. An elderly QA sister awaiting her turn to be served murmured, 'Don't forget a small oil stove and a kettle.' I thought she might be joking, but a glance at her serious face convinced me that she was not and, remembering the flat-iron which was included in my official list, I bought these extra articles. I certainly blessed my unknown adviser throughout the war years.

I suppose I must have had news of the war's progress, but it seems to have made little impression upon me. In the utterly strange world to which I now belonged, no one seemed to know for the immediate five minutes ahead just what they were to be doing next, let alone what they would be doing in the near future.

One morning, with two other sisters, I was walking past a door marked 'Matron' when an elderly woman came out.

Her scarlet cape was bemedalled and her voice was firm as she asked our names and wrote them down on a pad.

'Now, Sisters,' she began, 'I want you to go and take charge of the following wards ... The sisters have been posted away. I know how hard it will be for you with no one to help and advise you in your duties. I remember it well, for the same thing happened to me in the 1914–18 war. You must take up the burden and carry on. Go now, give of your best, I know you will not fail me.'

Stepping out, head high, Florence Nightingale herself would have been proud of me as I strode into the ward to which I had been sent. Most of the beds were occupied, and the men in them stared at me with interest. An orderly – though I had yet to learn that was his title – came towards me.

'You have no sister on duty,' I began.

He looked surprised. 'Two of them, Sister ... er, Miss.' He glanced at my civilian uniform – the Harrods parcel had not yet arrived. 'They are in the duty room.' He pointed to a door.

Two medical officers, two sisters, put down their cups of tea to stare at me in astonishment.

'Work in this ward?' the senior sister drawled. 'Well, I suppose we can find you something to do. Oh, yes, you could take the temperatures instead of the orderly.'

Deflated, I picked up a tray of thermometers as the orderly answered the phone. He turned to me. 'What unit are you with? Yes, that's the one. You are to report to the sisters' mess immediately.'

I hope someone remembered those thermometers, because I never went back to remove them from the patients.

The only reason for my sudden recall seemed to be that my Harrods parcel had arrived. Soon afterwards we were told to get ready for 'immediate travel'. Clutching the newly issued tin hats, gas capes and our hand baggage, we clambered into waiting ambulances.

In the unfamiliar blackout we were delivered to reluctant householders near the hospital. With a completely unknown companion, I stumbled up the unlit stairs of a small council house into an unlit bedroom. 'We've only one candle, and we need that down here,' a man's surly voice said. Daylight revealed a small room devoid of furniture except for the lumpy bed on which we had spent a restless, cold night. To our relief, transport arrived before we could finish the scrappy breakfast a cross woman placed before us.

That evening, in the welter of orders and counter-orders that seemed part of this new life, we boarded a crowded ship bound for France.

It was in a large hall near Cherbourg docks that our matron addressed us next morning. She was a roly-poly type of woman who, unlike most senior QAs, seemed to tumble into her uniform, but her instructions were of a kindly, sensible type.

'Go to a café and have a good lunch. Then come back here and rest. Take advantage of this, for we may have a long journey ahead of us. And buy yourselves some fruit, cheese and biscuits.'

In the hall there were few chairs, and I was glad of my new travelling-rug as I lay on the hard floor throughout the afternoon while we awaited the order to move out. It came suddenly, and we were urged to hurry.

Now eighty sisters do not move quickly or quietly, eighty being the complement for a 1,200-bedded field hospital. Thinking to save some of us from a wet walk along crowded pavements to the railway station, a French officer gallantly offered to escort us through some buildings. Unbeknown to him, these had already been allocated to French troops who, in all stage of dress and mostly undress, stared in amazement as we traversed their barracks.

The train was dark and dirty and had no corridors. Nevertheless we were very comfortable compared to the men of the unit, who were travelling largely in trucks designed to accommodate eight horses. Throughout the night the train rumbled on and continued through the next day. There were long queues for the '*Dames*' whenever we stopped at a station; and sometimes we halted at a siding where the cooks lit fires on the embankment and made 'char' on a big dixies. Rumour ran riot: 'The French were refusing to accept us,' – 'The colonel was in the driving cab forcing the driver on at revolver-point.' I never heard the truth, but in the early hours of the next day we climbed wearily from the train, moved across to a convoy of lorries and at the end of a short ride sank, most gratefully, into the hotel beds which had been allocated to us. Never had a bed been more welcome.

The sparkling seas and golden sands of Brittany greeted me when I stared out from a small bedroom balcony later that day. And then the orders started to come thick and fast. We learned that our hospital was to be housed in a nearby casino, as well as several hotels. The large hotel to which I was sent proved to be of international repute. Each bedroom had a luxurious *en suite* bathroom, plus ample cupboard space, although most of the original furnishings had been removed except for the heavy curtains and some chairs. The comfort of these was much appreciated. Then the heavy iron, army-type hospital beds were soon positioned.

As I hurried along the corridor of the first floor (this was my ward), a strong voice halted me: 'Sister! You should not be carrying all those pillows. Two are quite sufficient for a sister to carry. If you need more, an orderly or a fatigue man will be called to help you.'

The change from the female-dominated world of civilian life was tremendous. The QAs in each 'hospital' might be small in number, but we were treated with the greatest respect by officers and men alike. One word of complaint against a patient or orderly resulted in his severe punishment, whether or not it was justified.

Until some time later in the war years, our officer status was honorary. We wore no rank insignia, and although we were saluted – because of our wide-brimmed uniform hats, we did not return this courtesy. Instead we gave a gracious nod and smiled 'Good day.'

I was not alone in having to learn to reconcile my nursing ideas with military discipline. Most reserve sisters walked around muttering gloom and despondency, but after a few weeks even the softest of us was capable of a stern reprimand. 'Private So-and-so, today is the colonel's inspection, and I am telling you now, that locker will *not do!*'

Patients in civilian hospitals go home as soon as they become convalescent, but in the services one is stuck with the recovering soldiers until they are fit enough to be returned to duty. A ward of pampered convalescents will soon get bored and lazy, while morale drops to a low ebb, so we had to learn to nurse the sick patients and encourage the others to get back quickly into army routine.

Once again, I was fortunate in my 'senior'. She was a real 'character', brought back from retirement to help mould us into the required QA pattern. Tall, thin and angular, she strode at a measured pace throughout the rooms that comprised her ward, more often than not with a well-worn canvas bucket – containing charts and notebooks – slung over her arm.

'*She* doesn't mean to get caught short,' the men would whisper audibly after she had passed.

Whether or not she heard these remarks, I doubt if they would have made her turn an iron-grey hair, although her face, tanned by years of service in foreign stations, often broke into a mischievous smile. She had a quick sense of humour.

Born – as so many of the older QAs were – of a family steeped in service traditions, she steered me through the strangeness of ordering army diets. In civilian hospitals requests were sent in for many fish or chicken meals etc. Not so in the military scheme: food was ordered in amounts, the addition being done before the diet sheet was written up. New admissions had to exist on 'subsistence' for twenty-four hours, but a third of an ounce of tea, two of sugar, an egg, bread, butter and cheese were not easily served to a sick man, let alone a hungry chap with a sprained ankle. Much juggling had to be done at times to keep a contented ward. Wary sisters always managed to keep something in the cupboard, despite eagle-eyed quartermasters.

Our patients were mostly admitted with respiratory ailments due to the wet, cold weather. There were few surgical casualties except for the night despatch riders who suffered at the hands of enemy agents. (Wires were stretched across the roads which caused severe injuries to speeding motorcyclists.) Throat infections spread easily in crowded barrack rooms, and I seemed to spend a great deal of my time trying to ease the painful discomfort of quinsy sufferers.

Then, as the winter months passed, came worsening news from the war zone; there was an undercurrent among the traders in the town. There were differing orders; a spate of rumours.

About this time I had an accident. Climbing to a high shelf of a cupboard, I missed my footing and fell heavily, suffering a slight concussion as a result. All too soon I became a hospital patient, and when sufficiently recovered I was ordered sick leave and sent back to Britain, travelling by Red Cross train. There were signs of great activity on the roads as the train moved towards the Channel ports – not just of military movements but of civilians in cars loaded with baggage, country carts piled with furniture, sometimes with horses and cattle walking behind.

'Where are they going to?' I enquired of the senior sister as she made her rounds through the train. She paused for a moment before she replied, and I was to remember her words later. 'They are moving southwards, and I don't like it. Like many of them, I've seen it all before in the 1914 war. The battles are not going well for us.'

Back in Britain, the fear and preparations for invasion surprised me. The war seemed to be overtaking us fast. When, after my sick leave, I should have returned to my unit, I received orders to report to headquarters in

London, where I was promptly given another seven days leave and instructed to await further orders.

I went down to Sussex to stay with my aunt and was greeted by a sentry at the end of her road, where barbed wire was stretched right across, barring anyone's approach through the road to the beach. Having been mobilized before the outbreak of war, I had never been given a civilian identity or UK card, and my BEF pass did not please the sentry at all. A sergeant was called. Then a young lieutenant was notified, and it was only the timely, and most welcome, arrival of the jobbing gardener who had known me for many years that convinced them that I was not a German spy. Nevertheless, I was told to report to the police station in a nearby town next morning to obtain more suitable papers.

Even this journey was not without incident. I was regarded with suspicion by the bus passengers when, at two roadblocks, I had to explain my lack of an identity card. My grey and scarlet QA uniform seemed quite unknown to them. Then, just as we neared the bus stop close to the police station, an elderly man collapsed. While awaiting the arrival of an ambulance, I pointed out to the police that he had in his hand an empty bottle – which had obviously contained tablets. In gratitude for my help, they readily issued me with a pass that enabled me to cross the barricade into my aunt's road, where another sentry – a regular soldier – surprised his companions by saluting me. Obviously someone in that part of the country *had* seen a QA sister before.

To the annoyance of the elderly curate who lived near my aunt, I was soon recalled to duty.

'Such a pity,' he grumbled. 'I had just included you in my air-raid warden rota. I have only one person capable of working as a messenger in the entire road. She has good strong legs but you must admit that she – your aunt's maid – is a little slow in the head. Now, *you* could have solved some of my problems in that direction.'

He really needn't have worried himself, for within a few days my aunt, her maid, the dog and the cats all had to move out and, like the other residents of that road leading

from the beach, had to leave their homes in the hands of
the military.

Eventually my orders came. My new unit was a small
hospital based in a stately home in the South of England.
Staff was being increased to that of a field hospital, and as
all available bedrooms were already occupied, newcomers
were housed, dormitory-fashion, in the attics. We were
then ordered to purchase tropical kit, so back to Harrods
again. Up went our camp kit, and we tied stout strings
between the beams on which to hang a forest of white
uniform dresses. We packed and repacked, but for where,
we knew not.

'Good heavens!' the colonel exclaimed as he and Matron
paid a surprise visit to inspect our quarters. 'This is worse
than an Indian bazaar.'

On the day we left Britain I ordered that a box of
peaches be sent from the greenhouse of this ducal
property to my parents living in London. Peaches, when –
if the news was true – Hitler's forces were massing across
the Channel ready to invade Britain! How could we,
standing alone, possibly defeat his army?

I cannot remember how I came to be apart from my
companions, for we were confined to our quarters to be
ready to leave, but for almost an hour I stood on the wide
portico of that splendid house trying to print onto my
mind the sights and smells of the green rolling hills laid
out before me. 'You may never see England again,' I
muttered to myself. 'Remember this, remember this.'

That evening we crowded into lorries to drive behind
the men of the unit marching through the town to the
railway station. People lined the streets, cheering and
waving. Their smiling faces were blurred for me, for across
my sight streamed the burdened figures I had seen before
on the crowded stations, the sorrowful roads of France.

The journey took all night and the next morning. The
track had been bombed; there had been diversions: the
rumours sped along the train. Later that day at a Scottish
port we boarded a ship, the *Franconia*, and in darkness
sailed to join one of the big convoys that were to become a
part of the pattern of the war.

I shared a very nice cabin and bathroom with three other QA sisters, and on deck there was a reasonable amount of space, even if the chairs were scarce. For the troops the journey must have been a nightmare of crowded messdecks and swinging hammocks. There was no air-conditioning in those days, and when 'Darken Ship' sounded at sunset and all portholes were closed, the air below decks became stifling.

In the early days of the eight-week voyage we moved far out into the Atlantic to avoid the very real fear of U-boats. Thirty or more ships spread across the ocean is an unforgettable sight, and the manœuvring liners and merchantmen, with nippy destroyers fussing around on their constant patrols, was something to be wondered at as they zigged and zagged in unison. But when alarms were sounded and the convoy scattered, each captain choosing his own course to get away from aircraft or torpedoes; when the thunder of exploding depth charges and the rattle of gunfire roared out; and far off a ship flared on fire – these are memories hard to forget. Tin hats and life-jackets were our constant companions. Lifeboat drills and panic-bags became part of our lifestyle.

We neared land, but the vivid green vegetation and the sparkling waterfalls were all that we saw of Freetown as we sailed southwards. No shore leave was granted. At Capetown a few hours ashore gave us a chance to stretch our legs before we sailed on to Durban.

Docking here, we were overwhelmed by the city's hospitality. When it was known that the troops were restricted to the beaches, lorry-loads of people arrived, bringing with them picnic meals, baskets of fruit and cigarettes. Men gathered in small and large groups, and music and singing drifted across the sand. With several other sisters and medical officers, I was whisked off to lunch at a beach club and then taken for a drive to one of the beauty spots, 'the valley with a thousand hills'. As I stepped from the car, the grass both surprised and disappointed me after weeks spent on board ship, for it was stiff and harsh, so unlike our English lawns. The view was outstanding: mile upon mile of hills, as rounded as the tops of the native huts clustering around them; the calls of the occupants echoing about us.

The respite was short. Soon we were off again, sailing northwards along the coast of East Africa. The heat increased daily, and our white tropical uniforms stayed fresh for only a few moments. We had formed friendships, settled into little groups. Several of my companions were Roman Catholics, and for the first time in my life I talked – beyond a few conventional remarks – to a priest of that faith. He was a young Trappist monk, released from his vows of silence for the duration of his war service. He was a great character, and despite the fact that I was an Anglican I enjoyed his talks with us. Through him my lukewarm beliefs became stronger, brought me a comfort and an understanding of my own Church which has never left me and for which I still thank him. It was no wonder to me that in the following years Father Flynn became a legendary figure among the men he served in the Western Desert Campaign.

The pace became slower, keep-fit addicts missed out their daily runs, the classes and lectures on tropical diseases shortened and, except for those unfortunate to be on duty, the whole ship drowsed through the afternoon heat.

Taking my turn in the ship's hospital one night, I was mystified when the orderly, detailed to accompany me on my visit to some patients in isolation, picked up a pile of newspapers. He preceded me through alleyways in which nude men lay sleeping, preferring the floor to the sweltering heat of the hammocks in the messdecks. A newspaper which he draped across their sweating bodies led to different reactions. Some didn't stir, others started up in anger to roll over in embarrassment at the sight of me, their oaths richly increasing my knowledge of swearing. 'I've young daughters of my own at home,' was the only comment the orderly made as he collected as many of the papers as he could – ready for the next night.

That spell of duty was my first introduction to the glory of the Indian Ocean, surely the most lovely of all oceans. With only the night-watch alert, I could stand on the silent decks and stare at the stars hanging so low that surely an outstretched hand could touch them. For a few brief moments I could feel the caress of a soft breeze on my cheek, smell not just ozone but a hint of strange, spicy scents as yet unknown to me. From the waters parted by the ship's bow darted flying fish, while behind us streamed the glistening trail of phosphorescence, widening, widening.

I was almost overwhelmed by this wondrous spectacle until a ship's officer said sternly, 'No lifejacket, Sister? These are dangerous waters, you know. Too hot for you in the hospital, is it?'

'Yes, I'm sorry about the lifejacket, I'll get it. It is my break time and I wanted to have a breath of air, and this is all so beautiful at night.'

His sternness vanished. 'Incredible, isn't it? I have been sailing these waters for years, yet I never tire of the beauty. But right now these nights worry us – there are too many enemy craft around.'

I returned below to the stifling ward where my patients with their minor ailments tossed restlessly in trim white cots, and my thoughts turned now to other men – and women – shipwrecked maybe and lying on rafts, in lifeboats, on these same glorious yet dangerous seas.

In a fog of rumours and conjecture the days and weeks passed. We were making for India, definitely India, the old campaigners prophesied, and I was pleased, for India I had always longed to visit. Suddenly there were glimpses of land, and these same men shouted 'Egypt! It is going to be Egypt!'

They were right. Nearly eight weeks after we had left Britain, the ship anchored in Suez.

I had expected sand – everyone knows there is sand in Egypt – but I had not thought about sand that covered everything, a thin layer that filmed the skin, nose and mouth. We stood beside our baggage on the dockside in the full heat of the noonday sun. 'Keep in the shade, ladies,' a port official said as he hurried past. Shade: there seemed little enough of that here.

Later we moved into a train. The carriages were airless,
the seats hot and gritty. Matron came along, her hair
covered in a thin scarf – my first purchase, I thought, if we
have to take many journeys like this. Slowly we rumbled
over sandy wastes until the early evening.

Cairo welcomed us at the main station. At least that was
my impression when I saw the crowds of people massed
on the platforms. I realized my mistake when the lorries in
which we were sitting turned into the wide streets of the
city. People – I had never seen or imagined them packed
together like this, jamming the pavements, the roads. The
clothes were fantastic. Elaborate turbans towered above a
sea of fez and small embroidered caps. Smart city suits
showed drab among the press of nightshirt-like galabeahs.

The lorries turned slowly into the surging traffic, and
the convoy broke up. No line of vehicles could keep
station in such a mix of cars and animals. Chauffeured
saloons competed for space with camels, laden high with
cotton or untidy stacks of maize. Decorated taxis jostled
flat carts drawn by oxen or shabby, thin donkeys. On the
carts huddled groups of women, their dark eyes flickering
restlessly over their yashmaks. The noise was deafening –
men shouted, car horns blared and donkeys' cries shrilled
a descant to the snarls of camels.

Women, except those in large cars, seemed few and far
between and were mostly shrouded in shapeless black
draperies, but in a city of such frantic activity a convoy of
female uniformed personnel, unveiled, seemed to cause
little surprise.

Soon we left the crowded streets to drive over sandy
wasteland towards Heliopolis, where lights twinkled in
the evening shadows, for strict blackout was not then part
of life in Egypt. Once a royal city, Heliopolis had become a
wealthy suburb, and a former palace was now a first-class
hotel.

The lorries turned into the hotel's spacious grounds,
and here we remained for several weeks, enjoying the
luxury, the exotic furnishings, and testing our palates with
strange, spicy foods. The gardens were full of unusual
plants and shrubs, and I became fascinated watching the

Sussex, 1940: back home from France

Theatre nurses in
training, London, 1935.
At weekends we would
wash the walls of the
operating theatres

Babies Balcony, 1937: in the clean Sussex air we cosseted the
children

Girls Heritage, Chailey Clump.
The Princess Elizabeth Clinic for Tiny Babes.

43

Washing oranges for the mess, in Egypt, 1941. All fruit had to be steeped in 'Pinky' (permanganate of potash)

Stanley, my husband-to-be, in 1942. Whenever there was an opportunity we would dance

This hut was typical of the desert wards

Little comfort but . . . we had electricity by this stage

Jerusalem was enthralling . . . Eve and myself at the Dome of the Rock

Feluccas trading on the Sweet
Water Canal, our water supply.
Chlorination often turned our
tea a rare shade of purple

An off-duty gathering on a
rocky patch by our hospital, in
1940

Oranje, First Netherlands-Indies Hospital Ship, *en route* from Suez to Durban in 1942. The isolation wards were located on the top deck, once the nursery suite (X = my cabin!)

An established field hospital in Egypt, 1941. Mud from the River Nile enabled the bushes to grow

Myself and a patient in 1942. Sisters from other wards came here to be treated

Local labourers built camps and hospitals at the beginning of the war

Donkey power: the gangs chanted as they worked

banana tree with its huge, tattered leaves and the long stem of slowly maturing fruits tipped by a dark purple flower. We were welcomed at the swimming-pool by various European mothers and nannies, and morning coffee there became a regular part of our day. Most of the women and their children were in the process of being moved to South Africa as the war in the Western Desert worsened. Soon they and all the service wives had gone, and only nursing staff remained in the towns and cities. Of course, this meant there were plenty of escorts to take us to view the sights of Cairo and the surrounding desert.

The pyramids, the sphinx, the mosques and minarets of Cairo were not new to me – avid reader of travel books that I had always been, but to be crawling up the narrow track inside the Great Pyramid, to touch the rough stones, this was almost beyond my belief. The treasures from the Cairo Museum had been hidden away, buried, it was said, in a secret cave far into the desert, but one day, one day, I vowed, I would visit the Valley of the Kings, Tutank-hamun's tomb, and see for myself the famous wall paintings which told how life was lived thousands of years ago.

Meanwhile, to someone new to the Orient, there was the Al Muski, the tourists' bazaar, to explore, a place of wonder and mystery. Narrow streets of small, open-fronted shops where boxes of silver and copper were fashioned before your eyes, strings of amber beads holed and threaded, and tray upon tray of precious gems spilled for your delight, all accompanied by strong, gritty coffee in small glasses.

Most of the craftsmen were young. Working- and living-conditions were so bad that life was short, starvation and death always close; constant thieving was just another part of life. Beggars abounded in all the streets; lepers with clawed, fingerless hands and twisted grotesque faces. Women, their sickly babes hanging from flaccid breasts, pulled at our skirts as we passed, wondering whether the grey-faced infants were alive or dead. The mothers' cries of *'Muskine, muskine'* – 'We starve' – haunted me. Egypt was no place for anyone with a small purse and a compassion-ate heart.

Day by day the numbers of Allied servicemen in Egypt

multiplied. The news from the desert worsened. The peacetime military hospitals in Alexandria and Cairo were bursting, and rumours abounded that a chain of them would soon stretch from the Mediterranean to Suez. Daily we awaited news of a move.

One evening, walking with my friend Eve in the hotel garden, we met and chatted with our matron, who told us that a few of our unit would be sent to start a hospital. We plied her with questions until she asked if we would like to be part of this advance party, and this was how our names were soon on a movement order.

Air-raid sirens had become part of each evening, but little air activity came near us. Sandbags were stacked high around official buildings. With wide doorways and arches built for coolness, blackout was difficult, and electricity was switched off at source when the alarm was sounded. Our heavy baggage had already left and Eve and I were packing our hand luggage one evening when the lights went out and our preparations had to be completed by candle-light as we were to be off to an early start. By the light of a small candle we peered around our luxurious room for the last time.

It was cool next morning, with wisps of mist shrouding the beggars on the pavements. Too cool for me, for I had sent my topcoat ahead, and I shivered as the lorries drove us towards Cairo station. Yet I was warm enough when we stepped out of the train several hours later. Three camels brushed past as we looked around. The station was small, only two platforms. Beyond the rails ran a long, straight road edging a sparkling canal; except for two or three shabby palms, there was nothing but sand. The air was hot and dry.

'That is the Sweet Water Canal,' drivers from the waiting lorries told us. 'It's not very sweet though.'

How could it be? As we drove along, we saw that it served as bath, kitchen sink and sewer for the small groups of houses nearby, as well as being a handy spot in which to throw rubbish and dead animals.

Deserts are not all smooth layers of sand with camel trains traversing tall ridges sculptured by the wind, as artists would have us believe. Many areas are rocky, gritty places with unexpected soft spots and even more unexpected sandstorms and whirling 'devils'. On such an area our hospital was to be sited. And as, after a short drive from the station, we bumped back across the railway rails to drive away from the road, the drivers told us glibly, 'The Aussies and the Indians turned down this place – too much disease, they said, malaria and such – so we British had to have it.'

They drove us slowly into the hospital compound. At least there, far off, stood several tin-roofed huts, all around them mounds of bricks and building supplies, dotted here and there by tents. Gangs of Egyptian labourers chanted as they hauled at wooden crates. Women walked in files, door- and window-frames balanced nonchalantly on their heads.

Several medical officers and a bunch of orderlies came forward to greet us, and after a word with them Matron led us off towards one of the huts. 'Here are our quarters,' she said and pushed hard at the door – which then fell off. We were soon to learn that our particular gang of workmen were not the best of craftsmen.

Small rooms led off a corridor, the floors were of concrete – under a layer of sand, wooden shutters hung at unglazed windows, and the rooms were bare, except for a large hook dangling from the ceiling. 'That's for your mosquito net, or yourself if you feel so inclined,' murmured Eve from the next room.

Outside, water was heating in a large drum over a fire of rubbish, and a standpipe stuck up from the sand. 'We share the hot water with the MOs,' Matron said as she went to inspect the loos.

Quickly she returned and asked that the officer in charge of the building be sent for. 'These will not do for my sisters,' she informed the harassed man, as she pulled aside a flimsy hessian screen to reveal four wooden seats located over buckets. 'These will *not* do for my sisters. We require single cubicles, if you please.' And with the gracious nod that only QA matrons can achieve, she moved away.

That was the only concession to our comfort.

In the privacy of those small rooms we slung our
mosquito nets, set up our camp kit, made our beds and
learnt the problems of canvas baths. Sufficient space had
to be made to stretch out the wooden supports, then the
water had to be carried in by canvas bucket; after a bath –
knees to chin – the water had to be emptied by the same
method and the bath stood up to dry; it was all a fatiguing,
time-consuming process.

When the sun had set and we prepared to walk to the
mess tent, another problem arose, one that was to remain
with us throughout our stay there. Mosquitoes. We had
met and cursed them in Cairo but these attacking hordes
were unbelievable. They descended in a thick cloud. As
yet we had no oil for our hurricane lamps, so as swift
darkness fell we stumbled across the sand, one fold of our
large organdie caps veiling our faces, like a group of vestal
virgins. Mosquitoes prefer some people to others: even in
Britain I had suffered from their bites, so I felt destined to
be a victim of malaria, but that did not come until some
months later.

A routine slowly emerged in our lives as the hospital
grew around us, built to the established pattern of a field
hospital of 1,200 beds. Around the perimeter ran a wide
road which linked us with the railway crossing and the
main canal road. Down through the centre of the hospital
ran another road bisecting the lines of wards into two
divisions, medical and surgical. At the top end of the area
there was a hospital for officers and sick sisters, and at the
far end, near to the railway lines, our quarters and those of
the rest of the personnel were built. The administration
offices, X-ray, operating theatre, dispensary and laboratory formed another block, adjacent to the interior road.
Each section was known by an initial, each ward by a
number. The wards were well separated, but no paths
linked them: one walked, as always, over sand, which got
into one's shoes and scratched feet and ankles. Our
normal uniform shoes with their narrow heels were
useless; in no time at all everyone wore those of the flat,
crepe-soled, variety.

A ward consisted of two huts, each housing twenty-four

patients. Another hut with an office, kitchen and stores connected these two parts. At the back were the ablutions and loos (bucket-variety, of course). Nearby there was a standpipe tap, shared between two wards, and a soakaway for waste water. The ward furnishings consisted of beds with mosquito nets, small lockers, a few hard chairs, a table, a washstand with basin and bucket, and a sterilizer which had to be heated by the kitchen primus. Two chairs, a table and a wall medicine/drug cupboard stood in the office – usually termed 'the sister's bunk'. One hurricane lamp was issued to light each ward; the sister had to rely on her own lamp. Comfort for patients or personnel was not encouraged, it seemed.

As the huts were built, we moved in to help unpack and clean the equipment. Well packed as it had been, sand had penetrated to most of it. Day after day we washed and dusted and then frequently had to do it all again. The Egyptian glaziers had a strange way of putting glass in windows. They did not use putty, just four nails in the corners of the frames. A slamming door or shutter, and the glass flew out, and in poured the sand to cover a day's work. After some weeks of this, the workmen were brought back, the glass was removed and a thick, opaque covering replaced it which kept out sand and insects as well as the light.

Then, when the building was going really well, came the sandstorms. The local people said they were caused by the desert djinns angry because their land was being disturbed; weather experts spoke of records being broken by unseasonal weather. Who or whatever the cause, this I know – that we all suffered from those sandstorms. Gentle women turned into shrill-voiced vixens. Quietly spoken men shouted and swore. Slight arguments flashed into furious rows. The effect of a sandstorm on a group of normal people has to be seen to be believed.

All I know is that the desert-dwellers I saw on the films before the war seemed to understand: they just covered their heads and lay beside their camels until the storm blew itself out. Not us, oh no, we had to pretend there was nothing wrong, even when a tin roof, a plank of timber, twirled towards us. Eyes, mouth and nose filled with sand, it was a battle against the deafening scream of the dry wind to walk to the mess, only to find that the meal there was barely palatable under its layer of grit.

There were 'sand devils' too – strange, sudden eddys that centred on a line of washing or a pile of rubbish and whirled it up and away. In moments of fantasy I wondered what the Germans would make of my best mess dress, cuffed and collared in organdie, if the wayward wind that whisked it up dropped it as suddenly in their battle lines. Soldiers spoke of tents and equipment that these sand devils bore away, but I did not see anything so alarming.

Slowly the hospital took shape. Slowly too conditions improved in our quarters. Our nearest town was three-quarters of an hour's drive away, Cairo twice as far, and anyone who went in the daily ration lorry was besieged with requests. Sisters visiting the dentist came back loaded with lengths of material, fervently praying that they were the right colour and pattern. Medical officers were expected to select straw mats, lamps and oil stoves, whilst the driver handled a daily list of packets of coffee, tea and similar items.

Each evening we moved our chairs and our lamps into one room and, a kettle bubbling cheerfully, shared needles and cottons as we stitched at curtains and bedspreads. Packing-cases were treasured and with a great deal of ingenuity became rickety tables, lockers and even wardrobes.

The arrival of mail, a birthday or the opening of a new ward was cause for celebration, with much noisy chatter which was quite bewildering to the medical officers listening in the quietness of their nearby hut. Laughter over dull things like curtains, tea and biscuits?

It was late November when the first mail began to trickle through to relieve our anxiety as to what had happened to our families and friends since we had left Britain in July. We had no radios, and the Egyptian newspapers had been full of the terrific raids on Britain. With no replies to letters, even to cables, we had feared for them, and as a Londoner I had prepared myself for really bad news.

The letters told me of their safety. My parents had left London to join a relative in a safer area. My aunt had returned to Sussex after some weeks of compulsory evacuation. But there were great gaps in the family happenings, owing to none of the August letters reaching us, and of course many others were constantly lost by enemy action in shipping and aircraft. At least those first letters gave us a lift in spirits and made us think of what we could do in the way of Christmas festivities.

The colonel told us that the hospital was due to receive patients during January and that the rest of the unit would join us then. The padres who held joint services, C of E and Noncomformist in one tent (the RCs used another), suggested a carol service on Christmas Eve. We readily attended a few rehearsals – where the piano came from I do not know, and then we began to get more ambitious: why not a concert on Boxing Day? There was a sergeant who was a wizard on the piano, another who had been an organist, some funny men and a chap with a fine tenor voice. And couldn't the sisters do some dancing? Twenty sisters and few of them under thirty.

My friend Eve remembered that I had once told of attending ballet classes before I had taken up nursing and how I had helped in the dancing school. It was enough. In no time my name was on the list of artistes.

'I can't – it is years since I danced solo.'

'Then get some of the others to help,' was the reply, and four of the younger sisters agreed to it.

'Something simple,' I said to the pianist.

' "The Skaters' Waltz"?' he suggested, and for the next few days I hummed the tune as I dusted and polished beds whilst arranging a few steps.

Silk material was bought in a bazaar, four pastel shades and a silver-grey for me. Cut and stitched by some of the other sisters, the dresses looked quite good. An urgent request was sent to Cairo, and after a search of the city a pair of blocked ballet shoes reached me. I stitched on the ribbons and wondered how on earth I dared to dance before an audience after all the years without practice, and I could hardly do any of that on the concrete floor which now graced one end of the assembly tent – that would tear the shoes in no time. Never mind, the audience was our own gang, they knew our limitations, they would be kind.

My *corps de ballet* was not shaping well. Eve was a pretty girl, with a winning smile, and she was a good ballroom dancer – Eve would be all right. The second girl was convinced that, as long as she twirled her skirt and beamed, the dancing really did not matter. Number 3 was of rare beauty but possessed of arms that seemed to have extra angles to them, and she had little sense of rhythm. The fourth was a reluctant conscript and heavy footed, added to which she was a 'counter': '1, 2, 3; 1, 2, 3,' she sang loud and clear throughout each rehearsal. Well, they were trying hard, and heaven knew what I looked like.

Then one afternoon early in Christmas week the blow fell.

There was some widespread delay in traffic from the desert, and we were to receive 200 or so walking patients before the evening. My name had been on the board for night duty in the event of any emergency, but with so many patients another sister was also detailed. In the wards in which beds were being hurriedly made up, we found no furniture in the offices, so our first job was to carry from our quarters a packing-case for a table, our chairs, oil stoves and a kettle, as the ward primus stoves had not yet been uncrated. Everyone helped to admit the patients, who were a mixture of nationalities. The hospital looked as if it had been invaded by fireflies as people hurried around, lamp in hand.

I fixed up a party of German prisoners awaiting transport to the prisoner-of-war camp being erected near the Suez Canal. One of them seemed really ill – pneumonia, I guessed. He was very young and shrank away from me as I knelt by his stretcher. A drink was refused, though his lips looked parched.

'He thinks you are going to poison him, Sister,' an orderly said, and went on in a spate of rich Cockney, ' 'Ere, mate, let's see yer swaller.'

I turned to the other prisoners, one of whom spoke some English: 'You, tell him to drink.' Blank stares answered me.

Thinking of the word 'poison', I dipped a spoon into each cup on the orderly's tray and drank. Slowly, as I stood waiting, the Germans picked up a cup, took a sandwich, then ate and drank eagerly. This time the boy on the stretcher did not refuse the cup I offered. When the guards came to take the group away, he put out his hand and touched mine as if in thanks. My first prisoner patient, and he had been terrified of me. What had they been taught that they feared for their lives at the hands of a nurse?

One of my wards was filled with minor surgical casualties, Australians. Another housed a mixture of French and British medical patients. Some extra tents had been set up, and in one of them were eight Libyans, who, wrapped in their blankets, showed only a few inches of dark hair. They had decided to use their army-issue socks as a type of turban against the cold. 'They have been fed; just let them sleep,' was the advice of the medical officer.

There was a drug cupboard in my office but, as the attached keys did not work, I walked around that night with tablets in one pocket and a bottle of quinine in another.

It was not an easy night, and oh, it was so cold! December was not the time to be in huts intended for the Egyptian summer heat. Neither was it the time to be wandering around between huts and tents amid piles of building-materials and unmarked slit trenches, with only the wavering light of a hurricane lamp. There was no moon, so at least there were no air-raid alarms. By midnight all patients had been fed and were in their beds, and the day staff had gone, leaving another sister and myself in charge until 8 a.m.

The orderly came into the office. He banged down a mess tin on the makeshift table. 'I'm making some tea, Sister. You'll need it with this lot.'

'Tell the other sister, will you?' I waited until she came before opening the tin.

To my amazement she burst into tears at the sight of the food. She was Irish, with a rich sense of humour normally.

'What is the matter?' I asked in concern.

'All this way from home,' she sobbed. 'Here in this terrible desert, and all they give us to eat is some bread and a cold tinned herring.'

She was inconsolable, and as my oil stove was given to smoking, the unusual-tasting tea did little to cheer her.

We left the orderlies to watch and made our way back to our quarters, fearful of falling and dowsing our lamps. Here we put on another layer of clothes and, with our top-coats beneath our cloaks, felt better able to face the rest of the night. Something made me take back some candles, a lucky thought, as before dawn broke our oil supplies had run out.

I was to work many months of night duty in that hospital. Nights so busy that it seemed impossible to get through, nights so slack that time dragged, but none remains as clear to me as that first bleak night when the stillness seemed to press down and unseen powers of darkness stretch out with black, imprisoning hands.

I was afraid – of what?

There was a prayer on my lips, I knew not why, as I walked past the rows of sleeping men. I dreaded the future in this desolate place. Then, as I walked through the doorway of a hut, I looked up and saw the sky. The fears of the night left me, and they never returned. For this was not the slow, gentle dawn that I had so often watched in Britain. This was a time of magic, a moment that again and again was to cheer me after nights of worry and distress over sick patients, or fears for loved-ones at home.

Dawn in Egypt has a beauty of its own. Across the dark night sky, fingers of turquoise, green and coral tear away the purple clouds. The sky lightens and every grain of sand seems to shimmer separately in the pale glow. The wind stills, and for an instant the whole shining mass of land seems to creep forward, then the rising sun beams out, rolls upward in an orange ball, and another hot, brash day has begun.

By Christmas Eve things had become organized. As I

walked on duty, carols were echoing across the sand. By midnight there was silence as I went through the wards to place on each man's locker a box sent by the Red Cross and the Egyptian Red Crescent Society. Each contained a packet of stationery, a wallet of stamped leather, a comb, razor or similar toiletries. Some wags had pinned socks to their mosquito nets. At times like this I was glad I was a non-smoker, for my weekly issue of fifty cigarettes came in handy, and the tins were of inestimable use. A few loose cigarettes stuffed into those socks were my Santa Claus offering.

On Christmas morning the oil in my lamp ran out before I had completed the temperature round, so I used my last candle. Squinting at thermometers in such light is bad for the eyes and far worse on the temper, but I had to smile when I was presented with a gift. A thick stick and string, wrapped in silver paper from cigarette cartons and marked 'For getting 'em up.' A reference to the long whip carried by the ghaffir, the overseer, of Egyptian labourers and wielded with much show whenever anyone was watching.

My colleague was a Roman Catholic, and while she was at Mass I took over her wards and was greeted with more shouts of 'Merry Christmas!' Later most of the up-patients came to the service held by the C of E and Nonconformist ministers, and some stayed for Communion. The mood was good. 'Next year in England!' we said as we walked away – but had I not said that last year in France?

The men were still in good shape when I went on duty that night. They had had good food: pork, beef, Christmas pudding for dinner, cakes and mince pies for tea. The cooks must have worked hard, for they had only field ovens, as the cookhouse was not yet completed.

My worry now was the Christmas concert. 'Not dance?' The padres had looked in horror as we suggested cancelling our part in the performance as we had had so little practice. 'You must dance. These lads deserve some entertainment. There is no one else, so it is up to us to give it to them. Of course you are good enough; we don't expect Sadler's Wells standard.'

The tent was packed with men, and centre of the front row sat Matron and the colonel, flanked by most of the medical officers. The choir sang, the tenor, the pianist, and the violinist all did their piece, and then: 'The Sisters will dance for us.'

In response to this announcement, shouts and whistles broke out. To quieten them, the pianist struck a few chords. Regardless that the opening bars of 'The Skaters' Waltz' had yet to be played, the first of my *corps de ballet* (she of the beaming smile and twirling skirt brigade) bounded onto the stage, and – too inexperienced to wait for the right music – the rest followed, their steps badly mixed as they tried to pick up the music. The 'counter', coming last, gasped between her '1, 2, 3': 'You're all going the wrong way. You're doing the wrong steps.' The audience roared with laughter. Convinced that all was lost and that it was up to me to get them back into line, I made my entrance *'en pointes'*. In desparation I swayed and pirouetted in a way I had not thought possible on that concrete stage. Although it was not good ballet, the men quietened, watched and roared their approval as we made our exit.

After entering the first ward that evening I decided to leave the rest to the orderlies until all were settled. Men had leapt forward to strike ballet poses, and a trio perched precariously on a bed were using a mosquito net as a stage curtain. Next morning one of the wards presented me with a silver paper crown and wand. At least they had enjoyed our efforts, though one of the medical officers grumbled, 'Why did you not say you could dance before? We could have used you in France before ENSA came out.'

Later that week we had *our* Christmas dinner, and although there was a raging sandstorm, our two army cooks gave us a meal worthy of a first-class hotel, all cooked in a field oven near the mess tent. Matron welcomed us with sherry and other drinks and then, with the help of two orderlies, served the twenty present with turkey and all the trimmings and ran round the table with the Christmas pudding flaming bravely before we ended with dessert and coffee. Christmas 1940 – in the desert.

Some patients who were admitted later that week had a sorry tale to tell. As walking wounded, they had awaited transport by the roadside and eaten their Christmas dinner – a few biscuits and a small tin of bully beef.

5 'You must not let it get you down'

With the New Year, most of the unit's personnel joined us, and the builders had almost finished.

Around the perimeter of the hospital a line of civilian tents had sprung up. We had our tailor, shoe-repairer, laundry and a cinema – an open-air one, of course. The cinema was organized by Mr Shafto – known to all servicemen for his camp shows. The entertainment was unreliable: reels might be shown upside down or in the wrong order, sometimes part of a comedy would intrude on high drama. More often the projector failed and the performance ended prematurely.

The cane chairs were a breeding-ground for bugs and fleas, the whine of mosquitoes sounded shrill above the film voices, but we went there to escape into a world of fantasy. It was pleasant to sit relaxed, knowing that the worries of the day were now the responsibilities of someone else. When the show ended, the patients hurried back to their wards, those with an injured arm helping men with a limp, for the few wheelchairs we had were useless on the sand. We went to our quarters to brew tea or to the Bilharzia Arms.

This was a marquee erected between the sisters' and the medical officers' messes and was named after a disease prevalent throughout Egypt which is borne by water snails. Bilharzia ensured a course of unpleasant injections for anyone unfortunate enough to be soused in the Sweet Water Canal, often the result of driving a car or lorry off the road – easy enough to do on moonless nights, even easier when the moon was full and casting deep shadows at bends at which road and canal converged.

The marquee was open each evening and served as a meeting-place for us and our friends. Parked outside could be seen a variety of transport – cars, lorries, bicycles and, I have heard it said, even a pony and a donkey; anything, in fact, that could be begged or borrowed. Inside the tent we had a few chairs and tables, a gramophone and a limited amount of drink.

And now there was really something to celebrate, for electricity was to be laid throughout the hospital. At first it was only for the operating theatre and the X-ray department, but slowly it crept along, ward by ward. There was no power, except for specialized places, so the ward kettle and the sterilizer were still dependent on those wretched primus stoves. The lights did not stay on all night, and if the air-raid alert sounded anywhere along the Suez Canal, off went our lights. But those switches were like magic to us.

Almost better were the baths that now appeared in our quarters. Not your porcelain or enamel type – these were copied from a sarcophagus mould, I suspect, and made of some coarse, scratchy material like cement. But, lined with a towel, it was a bath, a proper bath. Why no showers were provided, I don't know.

The Young Women's Christian Association opened some small hostels for the use of sisters on days off or leave. (We were then the only uniformed women working with the services in Egypt.) The hostels were a haven of rest and more reasonable than the hotels open to us. The rooms were well furnished and near enough – or had transport – to enable us to reach a town for shopping and a hairdresser. The joys of flush sanitation and hot almond oil shampoos made life seem real again. At places along the Suez Canal the French had built clubs for the benefit of their engineers and families and open to us, in which we enjoyed swimming, good food and dancing.

I could understand why my family found my letters confusing. Either you write of long hours of work in fearsome heat, of oil stoves and leaking lamps, mosquitoes and flies, or you send descriptions of famous places, first-class luxurious hotels and glittering Cairo night clubs. 'We are bewildered,' they wrote.

Bewildered – they must have been, but so was my life then. It was as full of ups and downs as was the desert war. There were weeks when the patients were jubilant, talking of advances going well, weeks when 'retreat', 'retreat', was the only word heard. Tobruk, Mersa Matruh, Benghazi, the names were repeated over and over again. Commanders came and went, yet little seemed to be gained.

The men from Crete came to be nursed. They were low in spirits and full of bitterness for battles lost and comrades left behind, dead. Each ward had a radio now, so news, especially bad news, travelled fast.

The hot summer weather tried us sorely, for we worked normal British hospital hours, not the half-day sessions of peacetime. The heat started when we went on duty and had barely slackened by the time we finished. Mosquitoes, fleas and bugs left few areas of our skin free from inflamed lumps which itched by day and night and easily turned septic. One of our senior sisters had written a list, so she said, of those of us who should be put down as our incessant scratching threatened her sanity.

Weekly half days off were spent mostly in camp. We had not sufficient energy to make the long trek into town, either by hitch-hiking on passing military transport or by pre-arranged lifts. Such expeditions were left for nights or monthly days off.

Night sisters found it hard to sleep in the daytime, when they tossed restlessly on camp beds sticky with sweat, in airless rooms with shutters closed against the torrid sun.

Hard as it was for us, it was worse for patients rigid in plaster casts or shivering and sweating with fever.

Most wounds were treated by plaster casts. As soon as possible the medical staff cleaned the injury, packed the wound with gauze soaked in sulphanilamide and applied a plaster. The immobilizing of a limb meant less pain, for transport from battle areas was by ambulance, ship and train. Often an iron 'Thomas hip splint' was fixed beneath the plaster, so that fractures could be treated by traction, stones, rock or haversack serving to elevate the limb.

On their arrival at a static hospital, the plaster was

usually left undisturbed, hopeful that healing was taking place beneath. But the smell from the plasters grew steadily, and often we moved these patients out of the ward onto the narrow verandah, but because they were besieged by flies, the poor men had to remain behind their mosquito nets by day as well as night. I felt so sad for these men – they were so embarrassed, until finally the MO would yield to their pleas and have them in the operating theatre for dressing, X-rays and replaster.

Flies were never away from us. Egyptian flies are large, bloated insects with shiny bodies. One needs a free hand to brush them off as one raises a cup to one's lips or moves the food on a plate. They were an added horror for men trying to come to terms with the loss of a hand. Each week a competition was held in the unit for the ward which sent in the heaviest weight of dead flies – again those cigarette tins came in useful. We all tried hard but despite our efforts those flies' numbers remained legion.

Ants were less of a problem. Standing bed legs in tins of Lysol kept them from climbing up to patients with oily dressings. Floors washed frequently distracted but seldom displaced for long their marching files.

Crickets were my pet aversion. Their large, squashy bodies plopped down from walls and ceilings in the night hours or hooked themselves awkwardly into mosquito nets, as did praying mantis and stray locusts. We feared scorpions, for their bites are very painful, and we shook our shoes carefully before putting them on, but I seldom saw them, or snakes, once the hospital buildings were completed. Except for once …

Relief sister on night duty was not my favourite post – a different ward each two nights! This time I was looking after the small hospital for sick sisters, from our unit and those of nearby hospitals. I went on duty to find that a girl had been brought from a ship to await transport to another hospital. Her complaint, 'mental disturbance'.

'That is all we need,' I said with irritation. 'The hospitals full of wounded, and sisters go off with nervous breakdowns.'

'She will be no trouble. She has been sedated.' Day Sister

went on with her report.

The new girl was in the end room near a door which was always kept open. She seemed drowsy, so I settled her down early, as several of the others needed my attention.

It was about 1 a.m. when I heard a bell ringing furiously (each sister had a small brass bell beside her bed).

'Shush! Shush!' I ran into the end room. 'You'll wake all the girls up! What is the matter?'

A shaking hand pointed to the doorway. The moon was full, and moonlight in Egypt is bright enough to read a newspaper by.

'There, a snake! It came into the room.'

'A snake? Oh no, we have monster mosquitoes but the snakes have all been cleared out. Don't you fret, there are no snakes here. Have a drink and a tablet and then go back to sleep.' I flashed my torch swiftly round the floor. Torches were on issue now. 'See, nothing there.' I fussed around her and she soon dropped off to sleep.

'Restless at 1 a.m.,' I wrote in my report. 'Talked of seeing snakes, sedation repeated.'

The senior night sister copied my remarks for the colonel's report.

The other girls kept me busy and were all awake before I went back into the end room. 'Good morning,' I said brightly, one hand on the net to pull it aside. A slight rustle made me look up. Coiled around the metal ring at the top of the net was a fair-sized snake. The girl was still asleep as I sped out calling, 'Hussain! Hussain!' The two ward servants, elderly Sudanese men, looked up from preparing the breakfast trays, and a passing orderly, hearing my urgent cries, asked swiftly, 'Anything wrong, Sister?'

'A snake!' I gasped. 'A snake on a mosquito net!'

The servants ran for a forked stick, and the soldier grasped a broom. Hussain 1 gave the net a quick jerk, and the snake half slithered, half fell, onto the floor. Hussain 2 pinned it deftly with the stick, and the soldier dispatched it with the broom. They bore the body away in triumph.

'Breakfast already? I'm still sleepy.' Sister stirred. I

busied myself rolling up the net before I asked, 'Did you sleep well?'

'I had some frightening dreams, but then I usually do, these nights.'

I made no reply; and when I went on duty that night she had resumed her journey.

My friend Eve had been sent on sick leave to Alexandria following an attack of sinusitis. It was an old problem of hers, and the sandy conditions in which we lived were not helpful. I joined her for the last two days of her leave and we travelled back together.

I was thrilled by 'Alex' and envied the sisters there the fresh, breezy climate but not their work. In the pre-war hospital, whose naval personnel had been supplemented by an army unit, the strain was horrendous. Day after day the very worst of the casualties from the battlefields, too badly wounded, too sick to travel farther, were left with them and, despite their care, many died.

Eve took me on a tour of the city. We walked round the glorious bay where the air seemed so fresh that I almost skipped along the Corniche until we saw the men in their hospital blues limping past, saw ships with gaping holes and shattered masts and heard the sound of anti-aircraft fire, which sent us scuttling into shelter. Later we toured the small zoo, where the animals drooped in the afternoon heat, and away from the town we glimpsed the glory of the *mish mish* – the apricot orchards.

We had been saving up for an extravagant trip to Luxor. Now it would have to wait until later; our finances would not stretch to two visits, even if more leave came up. But there were memories of cool sea breezes, flowerbeds and hedges brilliant with red and yellow bougainvillaea to carry back to the drab hospital compound.

At least our unit was a kindly one, a happy place – if war years could bring happiness when thoughts were constantly winging back to folks at home, and mail was scarce.

Few of the unit had been posted away, so we had come to know each other well. Perhaps it was because of this

that our matron and senior departmental sisters considered our likes and dislikes, so that I found myself most
frequently working by day on the infectious diseases ward
and at night on the acute surgical. They knew too of the
friendship which Eve and I enjoyed, so our work often
coincided and we were able to take off-duty together.

Heavy nursing appeals to me – the old-fashioned 'roll
up your sleeves' kind, and although I had no fever
training, there had been plenty of infections that came my
way in the children's hospital, so the isolation unit was
much in my style. The ward was smaller than most,
consisting of two large rooms, eight beds in each,
separated by a series of smaller rooms, making the total
patients up to thirty and staffed by one sister, one orderly
and a native sweeper.

Jigsaws have always appealed to me, and sorting out
men with their different diseases into these rooms was like
an ongoing jigsaw. One large room was usually filled with
confirmed tuberculous patients awaiting passage to South
Africa. Routine X-ray of chest for recruits was ignored in
wartime, and latent infection showed up as the result of
desert conditions. At that time there were few cures for
TB; long months of bed rest in sanatoriums were the usual
treatment. For these men the good climate and plentiful
food in South Africa seemed the best chance.

The other large room alternated between diphtheria and
typhoid fever, usually the former. Diphtheria was always
with us in Egypt, and as immunization of children was not
yet prevalent in Britain, many soldiers contracted the
disease. The type of infection was mild in the early stages,
and with sore throats being a part of life in a sandy desert
a man could be slightly unwell for a week before he found
problems with swallowing fluids or could not lift his rifle
to his shoulder, because the toxins of the disease had
paralysed muscles. Once the infection had been confirmed by a throat swab, the man had to be evacuated to
hospital as a stretcher case, to spend the next three weeks
lying prone in bed, with a slow convalescence to follow to
prevent any cardiac troubles.

Seldom did eight patients with the same disease arrive

together, so there were apt to be empty beds in the large rooms and extra ones pushed into smaller rooms which held one or two beds. These rooms housed a goodly selection – measles, mumps, typhus fever, yellow fever, guinea worm, even once or twice leprosy in African troops. Only smallpox was excluded; that had to be nursed far off in a separate tent.

The nursing was of 'barrier' type; that is, a special gown for each infection, hands to be washed before and after attending to each patient. Easy enough with running water in rooms, and unlimited crockery, but very consuming of time and energy with water taps and soakways outside, tin basins in each room and with patients confined to their own areas, bedpans to be dealt with by bucket sanitation. Yet somehow we had no cross-infection, and most patients made speedy recoveries and fidgeted and fretted through the last days of their quarantine.

They did get bored though, as they had no contact with men from the other wards, and although we had the first of the radios given to us, we needed several so that all could hear. Reading-material was very precious, and as each room had to be fumigated (a twelve-hour job) whenever a patient was discharged in order that it could be used for some other disease, the paperbacks reeked of some noxious gas as they were for ever being put into the fumes so that someone else could read them.

All this care, and then one morning the men in the TB ward asked petulantly, 'Why do we have to wait till the afternoon to get our paper?'

I turned in surprise. 'I don't know. Most mornings I meet Abdul with the papers as I come on duty.' And surely the men in the diphtheria ward had been reading me bits about some Cairo riots from the *Egyptian Mail* as I made their beds? I walked down to them.

'You had some papers this morning. What has happened to them?' I looked around.

'Abdul picks them up before dinner each day. He says you complain if they are lying about,' came the answer.

I walked swiftly to the end of the ward to the patch of

shade that Abdul favoured for his noonday siesta. He was not there. Instead he was out in the sunlight smoothing with a large flat stone all the creases from a pile of papers.

Next morning, as was usual after a reprimand, he was waiting to present me with a small bunch of flowers – which I strongly suspected had come from the highly prized garden plot in a nearby camp.

In 1941 the news was rarely good. Rommel – 'the Desert Fox', as the men called him – seemed able to counter any advance. Patients coming to us, sick and wounded, seemed very dispirited, and it had its effect on us.

Often on day duty a man would bring out photos of his family. That was a signal for the rest of the ward to get theirs out too, and one moved from bed to bed listening, admiring. On night duty it was different. Sometimes when I asked why a man was sleepless, the worries would come pouring out – children proving difficult in strange, cramped houses, bombed out and living with relatives, elderly parents needing care, and flighty wives. I was too inexperienced to offer advice. I could only listen and wonder. Why did folks at home write in such fashion? 'We think you should know … if only you hadn't gone away … I can't stand living here any longer.' A man struggling to come to terms with disfigurement, loss of an eye, a limb, had enough to worry him.

It was bad for the British; for those in the Allied forces, whose lands were under German occupation, the anxiety was endless. On busy nights the physical strain on us could be great; on slack nights the emotional needs could be as severe.

I was in the 'jigsaw' ward one morning when the medical officer hurried in.

'We still have an empty room?'

'Yes. What have you got for me?'

'Nothing infectious.' I looked up in surprise, and he went on, 'Special order from the colonel. There is a lad with multiple wounds. He was being sent to a special eye unit but he is too ill to travel further, they are dropping him off here, and the CO thinks it will be bad for the other men if we put him in a ward.'

We hurried across as the stretcher-bearers arrived. I did what I could for an unconscious patient with appalling head and eye injuries, amputations and chest wounds.

The C of E padre came in. 'Can I help?' he asked. He was a gentle, kindly man who still seemed to carry with him the calm of a country parish.

'Yes.' All the bitterness I felt forced the words from me: 'Go down on your knees and pray that he dies quickly.'

He was staring hard at me as I left him alone with the patient.

The soldier was still alive, still unconscious, when I prepared to go off duty that evening. The colonel, elderly like the padre and with a very paternal attitude towards us, went in to the patient and then waited for me. 'I'll walk you back to your quarters. Are you feeling well?' he asked, looking at me keenly.

'Thank you, yes. I'm tired, but so are we all. We have had a busy spell lately. Why do you ask?'

'The padre came to see me. He was concerned about you, and so am I. It is not like you to give up on a patient.' He patted my arm. 'All you girls have been working too hard, need some leave. But you must not let it get you down.'

When I went on duty next morning, the patient had been moved on to the special eye unit, and in his place was a large marine whose swollen face and jaw were very suggestive of mumps.

As I have already said, ours was a very close unit in which people were individuals, not just names and numbers.

Leave did come, but at the wrong time of year for our Luxor trip, as all hotels closed there during the hot months. Instead Eve and I went to Jerusalem.

We set off on the night train to Palestine and had settled down comfortably in an empty carriage when we reached Kantara, where there was the usual lengthy stop. Two military policemen and an officer opened the door.

'Sorry to disturb you,' the captain said, 'but as you are

the only ladies travelling on the military part of the train, I shall have to give you a companion. The lady is under guard and there will be a sentry posted in the corridor. I don't think she will cause you any trouble. She is a European who speaks little English. Just call the guard if you have any worries.' He moved to go before casually adding, 'Oh, if she wishes to visit the toilet, one of you must accompany her.' Ignoring our queries, he saluted and went.

A middle-aged woman came in and took the empty seat opposite to me, covered her dark hair with a scarf, pulled a light jacket from a small case and seemed to compose herself to sleep. I could not see her face in the dim blue of the nightlight. What does a spy look like, I wondered. Had they searched that bag, her pockets? Suppose she pulled out a gun and threatened us – and the sentry – when the train stopped? What if she was not a spy? Perhaps a murderess?

I slept fitfully, waking now and again with these and other worrying thoughts. And I was sitting up, watching with delight the wooded hills, the green valleys through which the train was speeding, when the woman stirred and moved towards the door.

'No,' I said swiftly. 'No, you must not go out.'

'*Toilette*,' she replied, and repeated the word slowly as if to a child and opened the door.

'Guard! Guard!' I called, and to my relief a soldier came forward.

'Now then, now then – where are you going?'

'*Toilette*,' she repeated as she pushed past him.

I shrugged my shoulders and stayed put but the sentry would have none of that. 'Kindly accompany her, Sister,' he said, holding the door wide.

Grumbling 'This is a good start to a leave' or some similar remark, I followed the woman. Quickly she opened the toilet door and even more quickly slammed it, and I heard the bolt snap fast.

'Will she be all right? Suppose she climbs out of the window or tries to kill herself?' My mind was full of John Buchan's stories.

'Don't you worry, Sister.' The man shook his head. 'She's gone to take a shot of dope or summat – that's my guess. That sort don't kill themselves.' He leant back nonchalantly against the swaying wall of the corridor.

'Dope – is that why she is under arrest?' I queried.

'Couldn't rightly say,' came the answer, and it sounded as if he did not care much either.

It seemed ages before the door opened and the woman stood there. Her hair was neatly combed, and her nose, a rather pert nose, was freshly powdered. She looked a most ordinary woman, I thought, as I followed her back to our carriage. Evidently she knew the locality, because she put away her jacket and sat holding her bag, as shortly the train reached Jerusalem. As soon as the train stopped, a military policewoman opened the door, and with a nod towards us the woman stepped out. No gunfights, no fighting – *39 Steps* was not like this.

Eve, who, having been on duty the previous night, had slept soundly and missed all the excitement, urged me to hurry or we would not get a taxi to take us to the YWCA hostel where we were staying. No one ever told me who the woman was or her crime, so I am still wondering whether or not we shared the carriage with a spy.

Jerusalem enthralled me. The press of people thronging the narrow streets of the Old City seemed less frenzied than those of Egypt, the small boys and the beggars less pestering, and the air more perfumed by fruit and flowers than the foetid reek of Cairo. Maybe it was the climate that made the difference, for, despite the brilliant sunshine, there were cool breezes that threatened to blow off our small straw hats and ruffled the white skirts of our tricoline dresses.

Around us moved dark-clad Jews, their long, ringleted hair topped by huge fur-trimmed hats; small boys carrying school books walked beside them. Arabs sat before their open-fronted shops, their heads covered with checked scarves, fringed and bobbled, and tall, graceful women from Galilee swayed past, their long dresses embroidered across the bodice.

There were few tourists in Jerusalem in the war years,

but it was a favourite place for troops to visit when on leave, and many hospitals were sited there. Uniforms of all the Allied forces were to be seen everywhere.

The city, the countryside, were all that I had expected and more – it was the sacred places that I found more difficult to accept.

Eve was a quiet but very devout Roman Catholic, and our differing churchgoing had never been a problem. She had an introduction to a Franciscan priest who, as his contribution to the war effort, was willing to take men or women from the services around the Holy Places. Father Julian, an American, arranged to meet us most mornings.

Jew, Arab and Christian jostle each other in the old parts of Jerusalem, and the Christians divide again and again into Greek, Russian Orthodox and Catholics around the Sacred Places. I think it was the large, ornate altars, the dusty statues dripping with gold and jewels that overpowered me. I had been brought up to believe in a green hill with three stark crosses. I found it hard to relate that to these vast buildings. The mass of flickering candles, stale incense, throngs of people left me bewildered.

Our expeditions were carefully planned, and with Father Julian's guidance we travelled by bus or short taxi rides to Bethany, Bethlehem and Nazareth. Again the Church of the Nativity of Bethlehem shattered my childish faith with the magnificence of the manger marked by the gold star, and I was saddened to see the Muslim soldier standing guard to prevent the fighting that at times had broken out among differing Christian sects.

All was not disappointment though. The beautiful garden of Gethsemane, with its aged olive trees, the blue and gold onion domes of the Russian church nearby, and the Church of All Nations built over the Rock of the Agony were as I had expected them. We went back there alone one evening to hear Benediction, and the setting sun's rays shone through the glorious windowed ceiling as young choirboys sang familiar music with strange Arab tones. Of course, Father Julian did not take us to the Garden Tomb, as it was not accepted by the authorities,

but we went there on our own. It is said to have been
discovered by General Gordon and is a rough-hewn tomb
as it would have been in the time of Christ.

A strange thing happened on that holiday. I had for
weeks suffered from a very irritating rash, mainly on my
hands, the result of an infected bite. Treatment had eased
it, but return to duty and frequent handwashing had
caused it to recur again and again. On the day we had
booked a trip to Jerico and the Dead Sea, it was bad
enough for me to cover the palms of both hands with
bandages. We spent so long splashing around in those
strange salt-laden waters that we had to hurry to catch our
coach back to Jerusalem. Eve wanted to change the
dressings on my hands.

'We haven't time,' I said. 'Never mind. It is so hot, the
gauze is almost dry already.'

A delay on the road caused us to be so late that there
was no time to change before we went out to a concert for
which we had tickets. At the end of the evening I was too
tired to do anything about dressings. I just fell into bed.
When the bandages were removed next morning, it
seemed like a miracle – the salty minerals of the Dead Sea
had done what modern medicine had been unable to
achieve: my hands were completely healed, and from that
day, with care, I had no more trouble with them.

On Friday, the day before our return, with some other
parties we walked the Way of the Cross. There were few
tourists, of course, but their numbers were made up
largely by troops of all nations, mostly on leave, though a
few were stationed in Palestine. How right they seemed to
be in the procession as we moved, with a stop at each
place at which Christ had halted, on the route along which
he carried his cross to his crucifixion. Roman soldiers
would have been there, jostling the spectators as they
hurried with orders or provisions for their guardposts.
Grumbling shopkeepers would have moved or covered
their goods as the crowds pushed past in the same way as
they did now, and unbelievers would have sneered and
shrugged their shoulders as some people still did, as a
procession nearly 2,000 years old passed by.

Among a group of nuns, priests and devout pilgrims were some men carrying a large wooden cross. So many nationalities, so many facets of one faith. I was – I am – glad that I walked the Way of the Cross.

We said our farewells to Father Julian. He blessed us and gave to me, as well as to Eve, crosses and crucifixes blessed at the Holy Sepulchre. We gave him tobacco, the only gift suitable to a besandalled priest in the brown habit of a Franciscan.

The battles started up afresh, and many of our British orderlies were sent up to the fighting areas. They were replaced by Italian prisoners of war from their medical corps. They were housed in a camp adjacent to the hospital and were eager to work, as it gave them more freedom. They were allowed to wander anywhere in the hospital during their duty hours, returning to their camp only for meals and to sleep.

The great problem was one of language, especially when our staff was increased by a unit of Jewish ATS. These women were largely refugees from occupied countries who had managed to escape to Palestine; Polish, Finnish, Hungarian, their common language was Hebrew. Some were highly educated professional women, but with no credentials to back up their claims. Many spoke several languages, and these were employed in the administration offices, pharmacy and laboratory; others with no skills worked in the cookhouses or on the wards.

Speaking none of their languages, nor Arabic, we had to explain the work largely by hand signals, the patients helping out with army slang. It is not surprising that our speech became a jumble of badly pronounced Italian and Arabic. One no longer had a look at a wound – one took a *'shufti'*. The morning was *'bella'* or *'quiess'*, and there was always *'maleesh'*. *'Maleesh'* typified Egypt: 'It doesn't matter,' maybe. A lift of the shoulders, a sideways nod of the head and – *'Maleesh'*.

In these circumstances it did not need a sandstorm to make one frustrated. A wide-eyed look of bewilderment from an ATS girl as you asked her to take a specimen to the laboratory, a puzzled shake of the head from an Italian POW told to fetch kit from the stores, could drive a busy sister to distraction. As always, the patients came to our aid. Some up-patient would come to the rescue with 'Come on, Miriam [or Toni], I'll show you,' and would lead them off, shouting loudly and frequently their destination.

Some POWs were excellent and had served in Italian hospitals. Some were appalling; these could be sent back to their camp. But mostly, with supervision, like the ATS girls, they worked very well.

Kit was one of a sister's nightmares. Some patients were admitted complete with full kit, others arrived with not even a toothbrush. As soon as they were allocated a bed, they undressed and their uniform was replaced by hospital blues – blue trousers and jacket, white shirt and red tie, grey pyjamas. All this had to be collected from the stores, and all uniform and equipment handed in. Very fine if the patient was fit enough to do it for himself, but a tough job for an orderly if he was not.

Rifles and such were the first things to get out of the ward. A wise precaution with the mixed nationalities we had to deal with. I once walked in and found two men throwing knives at each other across the ward. Such arguments did not go down well with me, as that Cypriot and Turk found out very quickly. It caused me to have any further Cypriots searched on arrival, probably most unfairly.

Up-patients whose medical state was sufficiently good were put on 'fatigues' (certain duties) each day. These included helping to fetch and carry meals and stores from the cookhouse or collect fresh linen. When convoys were frequent, these fatigue men grew fewer. The policy was to bring patients to us after they had received treatment at the casualty clearing stations, and then as soon as possible we passed them on to hospitals in Palestine. The more pressure on our beds, the quicker we sent them on, retaining only the dangerously ill patients. Orderlies were then kept hard at it on routine tasks, and sisters could not rely on them for nursing care. With no visitors, relatives or volunteers to help, everyone had to pull their weight to keep the men clean, fed and comfortable.

Our matron, an elegant lady who well deserved the high office which she later achieved, was a born administrator. In the early days she watched the handling of a convoy and drew up a plan which was then used in most desert units.

Men walked or were carried into the big assembly hall or marquee, where they were quickly seen by medical officers, who, with the help of Matron, padres and staff, checked the casualty card worn by each man. Tea, sandwiches and cigarettes were offered and wards allocated. All staff members were on duty, so patients were soon by their beds, where ward sisters waited to admit them. This method proved far better than the previous one of not feeding the patients until they were in their beds. Tea, eggs and fried bread were great for those who could keep awake, but most longed only for a bed on which to sleep after hours, or days, of jolting painful travel. And the food was often wasted after the cooks, poor souls, had been roused to prepare and cook it following a hard day's work. Sleep was the best cure we could offer; proper meals could wait until the next day.

There were some additions to our comfort as time went on. The sand between the medical officers' and the sisters' messes was levelled and a tennis court marked out. No Wimbledon stars emerged but it was a source of exercise when the heat and storms permitted.

The Red Cross purchased some small Ford trucks which were given to the desert hospitals for the use of the sisters. Finding a suitable driver amongst the troops whose category prevented his being sent to the battle areas, and arranging fares to cover his wages, petrol etc., took some time but was finally settled. A scheduled programme of trips to the city or the nearest town was established, and for six of us at least there was no need to seek lifts from nearby units, wait for camp buses which frequently forgot to call for us, or walk to the road to hitch a lift on whatever uncomfortable lorry or other army transport came our way.

I was very lucky from the transport angle …

One night a patient was admitted to one of my wards. He had a severe wound of back and shoulder and looked very ill. I saw him settled as comfortably as possible and gave him some sedation. The convoy was a large one, and patients were spread over several of my wards, so I was fairly busy, yet I felt a vague uneasiness about that particular man. Later, as I was walking to another ward, I had one of those strong feelings that used to alarm me when I was nursing small children. 'There's something wrong. Go back and look.' I turned around. The orderly was standing by the door and said in answer to my enquiry, 'He does seem a mite restless.'

The man only nodded as I asked if he had much pain, but when I put my hand beneath him to lift him higher, I found he was lying in a pool of blood.

As the orderly ran off to fetch a medical officer, I snatched open a dressing-drum and packed a whole roll of gauze into the leaking wound. They kept the poor chap down in the operating theatre for most of the night, fearful that the jolting move back across the rocky paths might finish him. He looked scarcely alive when he did return, but he seemed to be holding his own for three nights, and then the episode was repeated again, and three nights after that. Each time I did not expect him to return from surgery; each time he did and finally made a good recovery. No doubt I spoiled him, starting each night with a special hot drink when I gave him sedation, and a quick word as soon as I went on duty, but he was a sick man and I needed to reassure myself against further alarms. Soon he was well enough to leave for convalescent camp.

A few weeks later I went to the transport depot in Cairo in the hope of arranging a lift back to hospital. I received a great welcome, for there he was, in charge. After that there were no more trips back for me on an old oily ten-ton lorry. Somehow a car, a small truck, could always be found that – maybe with a slight deviation from its planned route – could take me back. Those grateful patients – how in their turn they helped us!

Eve collected boyfriends more easily than I, an avid
reader, collected books. She was always enlisting my help
to placate one of them, pass on a message or try to explain
why she had broken a date. It was on such an errand that I
went across to the Bilharzia Arms one evening. It had been
a long day and I had no intention of staying there until an
officer detached himself from a group from a nearby
camp.

'Hello, Sister. We have met before.'

I stared without recognition. 'Do you remember the
concert on a wet evening in France?'

France! It seemed years ago, that civilized world we had
known before this nomad-like existence. I thought hard
before I said, 'Of course, that big effort put on by the
French Red Cross. Oh, were you the kind man who lent
me a coat as we ran through that streaming rain?' I could
be forgiven for forgetting him, for I had had only a glimpse
as we hurried from the theatre to lorries waiting in a
nearby field. 'I don't believe I thanked you for that coat –
and you must have got soaked without it. It was kind of
you.'

'Our only concern was to get you girls away before the
lorries bogged down.'

We sat and talked. His name was Stanley Parkin, and he
was Regular Army. Our war service seemed to have had a
similar pattern. France, a few weeks at home and then
Egypt. He had been 'up in the blue' (why did they call the
battle areas that?), now he was at a nearby camp, starting a
new workshop.

'A good posting, one you enjoy?' I asked, thinking of
the number of camps and workshops that seem to be
spreading towards us from Cairo itself.

'Yes, I enjoy starting new ones.'

An officer I knew came across from a neighbouring
table. 'So you two have met?' He sat down beside us. He
was a quiet soul, one of many whom war had made into
an unlikely soldier. 'He is keeping me in order,' he
confided. 'Very regimental, our Stan. He even gets his
native workmen lined up in straight files – it is one of the
sights of the camp.'

I accepted an invitation to a forthcoming Christmas party at their unit. As I said goodnight, I had no inkling that this chance meeting had changed my life.

Christmas, and my poor men in the 'jigsaw' ward were not looking forward to it with anticipation. Measles, mumps and typhoid fever are not welcome guests at festivities. Concerts, singsongs, even church services were denied them. Their Christmas dinner would be a good one, but sandwiches and buns for tea were hardly exciting. Even if I bought and made some jellies, they would not set – the supplies of ice for our ice-box were very unpredictable, and did grown men like jellies? All I could do was to string some tinsel between the mosquito nets.

It was having a sergeant cook patient in the ward that had given me the idea. 'What we want,' he'd said, 'is a good old-fashioned sherry trifle.'

'And you shall have one,' I replied without even thinking. Well ... anyone could make a trifle when they had a day off in Cairo to buy supplies.

Cairo is renowned for cakes with lots of cream and brittle spun-sugar icing. Plain sponge cakes suitable for trifles were not available. Nothing daunted, I returned laden with flour, sugar, cherries and silver balls.

In the ward kitchen there was an ... an *object*, used, it was said, by the night orderly to warm up his meal. A sort of oven that fitted on the primus stove.

Everything was organized so that I should be off duty on the afternoon of 23 December. The sergeant cook in the far room called out the instructions from his bed, which were then relayed to me by various men in turn who were sitting in the doorways of their rooms. From the Geordie with the mumps, they were really anything but clear, but I soldiered on.

The primus, especially cleaned, was burning brightly and the oven seemed quite hot. Five mess tins were greased, and Abdul, the sweeper, watched me from a corner, absolutely fascinated, as I beat up the eggs he had procured for me (no doubt at a handsome profit). Into the tins went the mixture. Into the oven went the tins, and we all waited patiently until a chorus of *'Time!'* came from those with watches. Sadly I reported that the cakes looked very pale and soggy still.

'Give them another five minutes and pump that primus up,' the cook's instructions came back.

We never reached that period of time. Suddenly there was a roaring sound, the oven door burst open and thick, oily smoke belched out in all directions. Abdul, with frenzied cries to Allah, made a very hurried exit.

Unfortunately my ward was near the admin and guard huts, and the sentry, hearing the pleas to Allah and seeing the smoke, seized on this as a diversion for a dull afternoon and beat a loud tattoo on the brass triangle that served as the fire alarm. Within minutes, the colonel, the wardmaster and their staffs, the fire piquet and anyone else with time to spare came running, calling for buckets of sand and water, as they ran.

With tears of frustration pouring from my smoke-filled eyes, I assured everybody that the fire was out. So too were the cakes! They were splattered all over the walls and floor, making a truly Christmas feast for the armies of ants and crickets already converging on the sweet, sticky debris.

Next morning a truck pulled up outside the ward. A sergeant (an ex-patient) got out. 'Happy Christmas, Sister,' he greeted me with a broad grin. Then he went on, 'We heard you'd had a little problem with some specialized cooking.'

'You and half the Middle East!' I retorted quickly.

He laughed aloud. Evidently the story had lost nothing in the telling. In fact, it had probably gained some embroidery. 'Well, it's like this, Sister. We are having a bit of a "do" in the sergeants' mess tonight, so we made a few bits extra for your lads.' And out of the truck came sausage rolls, patties, scones and cakes and, last of all, a huge bowl.

He brushed aside my gratitude. 'It's nothing. Nothing at all. Just a "trifle" of goodies ... for Christmas.'

Malaria nearly ruined the plans Eve and I had made for our visit to Luxor. To say nothing of its spoiling the carefully kept charts of our malaria officer.

This MO and I had clashed before. Unlike most of his colleagues, who left the diet sheets to the ward sisters' judgement, he insisted on poring over them each day. No small items, such as eggs, two ounces of brandy or a tin of milk, escaped his notice. Pleas that they were needed for the small emergency supply that all sisters kept went unheard.

To have developed the variety of malaria as yet not shown on his chart, and at the wrong time of the year, seemed to put me in the criminal classes. I was submitted to lengthy questioning and was left feeling that I had disgraced not only the unit but the whole battle campaign. Visitors of such type are not the best to ease the fatigue and depression left by a bout of malaria. I survived the required days on duty before I could be granted leave and left with Eve one afternoon feeling distinctly tired and limp.

Somehow we had scraped together enough money for a seven-day Cook's tour (troops were allowed very special discounts). This tour started from Cairo's main station, which, with its milling humanity, is enough to deter most people from travelling further. However T. Cook's has always been a name to impress, and soon we were settled in an elaborately furnished sleeping-carriage which, according to the attendant, had been used by 'royal' persons.

Our hotel in Luxor facing the wide River Nile was palatial, an oasis of coolness after the fearsome heat outside. Large fans rotated slowly overhead, smaller ones whirled and hissed from corners, and a cold drink appeared at the lift of a hand. My flagging spirits began to revive me, and – to my secret dismay – hotel meals put back the pounds the fever had stolen from me.

We toured Luxor town, visited the temple and then joined a tour to Karnak. This huge group of ruins lies on the eastern bank of the Nile, for the ancient Egyptians believed that was for the living, the western bank being kept for the burial of the dead.

If the pyramids had impressed me with their

magnificence, the Temple of Karnak overwhelmed me. The size, the grandeur of the pillars, still standing after thousands of years, the glory that there must have been when roofs topped the lotus-carved columns and shielded the sun from the immense statues of Rameses. Even broken and defaced as some of these now were, their majesty was undiminished. I forgot the heat, the buzzing insects, the chattering folk around me, as I listened to the singsong voice of the guide telling the history of Karnak. I was loath to leave, but the noontide heat drove us back to the comparative cool of the hotel.

That evening some officers dining at a nearby table invited us to join them on another trip. 'Karnak,' they said, 'like the Taj Mahal, is best seen by moonlight. We have booked some men and donkeys. The moon is full tonight.'

Eve tried to plead weariness but I persuaded her to go, and how glad I was that I did so!

By day the shadows cast by Karnak's ruined walls had been dark enough; in the moonlight they lay like black pools. The seated figures of the pharaohs loomed above us, their power and authority seeming to stretch out as if to surround us. There was a stillness broken only when a stray breeze scattered a loose handful of sand.

Walking through the avenue of crouching animals that line the entrance, seeing the gleaming stone, the deep shadows, I felt a sense of timelessness. Here joy and sorrow, birth and death, spanned the years. Here among the bowing priests, slaves had toiled and died; there had been giving in marriage, the loving and the hatred. Nothing was new in this place, nothing was old, and our lives, our battles, were only a moment in history.

Near me, half hidden by the shadow of a pillar, stood a man, his shoulders shaking. I had heard the officers with whom I had come speaking quietly of him: 'Poor bloke, he has just heard that his son, a youngster, is dying of cancer. God knows if they can get him home in time.' This was no place for platitudes, emotions here ran high, all I could do was to grip his hand and say, 'It is time to go now. The others are waiting.' I never knew his name, never saw him again, but war time is like that: a touch of the hand, a compassionate look, is all that time allows.

On the next day Eve and I rode donkeys out to the Valley of the Kings on the western bank. We walked down the deep passages whose walls were a vividly painted history of the people who had once lain within these tombs. We gazed upon the glorious gold mask of Tutankhamun, heard of his short life, the glory of the treasures found within his tomb. Fascinating, secret places where every step seemed a desecration of their rest, places I had longed to see – but how deeply I regretted the war that enabled me to see them.

That was the last leave that Eve and I shared together, as she was posted to a hospital ship sailing the dangerous waters of the Mediterranean. I missed her greatly; our friendship had been such a happy one. I was glad that Lieutenant, soon Captain, Stanley Parkin was able to take me out sometimes to break the monotony of camp life.

6   The tide of battle

The hospital was going through a quiet spell. That is, there were no nightly convoys by train from the battlefields; only small numbers came, and those mostly by ambulance. Most of our beds were kept occupied by men from the surrounding camps which seemed to grow in numbers every time I went along the canal road. I was working on the medical side, with the 'jigsaw' ward, malaria and dysentery patients. The days were filled with the constant feeding of fluids, tepid sponging (we could never say they were cold) and the collection of specimens for the laboratory. I do not recommend dysentery as a disease of dignity.

There was a strange feeling amongst the patients. Rommel was still up to his tricks, and our commanders seemed unable to get his measure. Were all the new troops flooding in from home, and our allies with new guns, new tanks, going to make the difference? The old hands shook their heads: 'You've got to know the desert first. They haven't got their knees brown yet.'

The German Army, my patients held in healthy regard; the Italians they dismissed with contempt. Somehow I think the mood then was one of apprehension.

Stanley and I shared a passion for ballroom dancing. He was of medium height, which suited my short stature. He was very slim, blond and with a quick smile which lit up his rather serious face and wrinkled the skin around wide-set eyes. He talked frequently of his family home in the north-east of England, an area quite unknown to me.

And whenever there was an opportunity we danced – on wooden or concrete floors, and sometimes even managed a trip to one of the Suez Canal clubs for a swim, dinner or a cinema.

But his life was in workshops, where vehicles of all sizes, guns and tanks were made ready for the battle that would have to be fought to stop Rommel and his men.

I realized very soon that Stanley was a perfectionist. His workshop, his men must be better than the rest. Perhaps that was why 'Recovery' came his way. It was a posting to the battle area. He didn't explain clearly to me what 'Recovery' was, so I asked my patients. 'Dicey job,' they answered, 'very dicey. They go into minefields and such to bring out tanks, guns, vehicles, even planes, ours or the enemy's, for patching up or spares.'

Stanley was up in Cairo for a short while, and we had one grand day there together. For once I was able to return some of his hospitality by taking him to lunch at the YWCA. A lovely old Cairene house had been taken over as a place where servicewomen could entertain their friends, male or female, of whatever rank. (This was most helpful if boyfriends or relatives were of 'other rank' status and could not use the hotels open to us as officers.) The house, once used by Egyptian royalty, was very spacious, with a large, pleasant garden. At the head of the stairs a huge, wondrously carved wooden screen had shielded the female occupants of former times from the gaze of the men in the assembly rooms below but gave them a fine view of all that was happening down there.

We had tea at Groppi's, the famous teashop. Having chosen from that spectacular array of cakes, we went out into the garden to watch the elite of civilian Cairo in their beautiful dresses (one day would *we* be out of uniform?), Groppi's Light Horse (that much-maligned group of officers working at general headquarters) and the extraordinary mixture of uniforms of many nations. There was no time for dancing, as I had the journey back, and there were no more meetings, for Stanley soon went 'up into the blue'.

I had promised to write to him, and I did, telling the

local camps' news and that of the hospital. Sometimes he
replied, saying little except that only boredom interrupted
the long hours of work and noisy times of sleep.

With the increasing heat of summer, the pace of work
quickened, as did the worries of the men. 'They are
getting too near Alexandria. Let them get along that road
and there will be no holding them. You girls had better get
your running-shorts ready.'
      There was typhus fever around too. With three other
sisters I was kept innoculated against the disease so that
we could nurse any suspected cases. With no drugs
known then that would cure the disease, one watched as,
after the appearance of the rash, the patient grew more
and more ill and less conscious of his surroundings.
      One of our sisters developed typhus, and I was sent to
'special' her at night. Each time I went on duty she seemed
more and more remote, taking even hours to give an
answer to a simple question. Her temperature, like our
anxiety, mounted steadily until the dreaded fourteenth
day, when either it would come down with a rush or we
would lose her. I left her that morning, a very sick,
exhausted girl. She was still ill and exhausted when I
returned in the evening, but her eyes were open in
recognition, and there was a ghost of a smile around her
lips. Her convalescence was slow but she made a complete
recovery. It is at times like these that I thank God I am a
nurse.
      Eve wrote to me that they were having their share and
more of air attacks, despite all the Red Crosses painted on
the ship. But she sounded well, and I laughed at her
account of trying to deal with three boyfriends at once.
Currently one was an MO on the ship, the second a
patient aboard and the third an officer in transit with
them. At least life afloat had not altered her.
      I went back to the surgical wards, which were now busy
with battle casualties, and my guardian angel surely
smiled on me when he sent a most unusual orderly.
      He was middle-aged, and his flat, shapeless feet
prevented him from work in battle areas. He could barely

read or write, and all medical terms seemed beyond him,
yet if I saw him struggling towards me on his poor aching
feet, I stopped and waited. 'I am sorry to bother you,
Sister,' he would begin in his slow way, 'but there is
summat about that poor man in bed 3 that ...' I never
waited to hear any more. I just ran. He was always right.
He could not take a temperature or check a pulse but he
knew when a man was near collapse. He was no practical
use to me in a crisis – he could not understand why I was
trying to lift a bed onto blocks or dress a leaking wound,
but he would take the patient's hand and say in his soft
voice, 'Rest easy now, chum. Sister's seeing to you. You
will be all right.'

I asked him once what his peacetime job was and he
answered, 'Gravedigger and sexton in our fine old
church.'

With him on duty in a ward, I knew the men would
have simple, kindly care, and if danger threatened, he
would come and warn me.

There was a change of mood among the men coming
down from the desert. They had a new commander –
'Monty', as they called him. Stanley's last letter had said it
might be a while before he wrote again: 'Things are
hotting up and this new man keeps us at it – he is a fine
bloke.'

Invitations to camp parties along the desert road
became few and far between. The workshops were hard
pressed, and the patients admitted from them with illness
or accident seemed content to sleep for a day or so. They
spoke of having to work harder, faster, than ever before.

Coming off duty one morning, the quartermaster met
several of us with a request from the colonel that after our
meal we go down to the road and stand there. We said we
were tired, that it had been a busy night, but he assured us
it would not be a long wait and that someone very
important would be passing. Rather reluctantly we did as
we were asked. A convoy of cars sped past in a cloud of
dust, and then one reversed towards us. From the back
seat a hat was waved, as was a hand holding a big cigar,
and the car moved away.

'At least,' said the colonel later, 'you can tell your grandchildren that Winston Churchill stopped his car to wave at a group of nurses standing on a spot where no sane person would expect a hospital nurse to be.'

Anyone who went to Cairo then came back with a grave face and tales of smoke and flames coming from the chimneys of general headquarters, of flakes of paper floating around the grounds. 'There is a real flap on now. They are burning papers night and day.'

Leave was cancelled and trips away from camp were discouraged even on half days. Yet the incoming patients spoke with a new confidence: 'This chap Monty, he's really stirring things up,' they told us.

On duty at night there seemed fewer and fewer empty beds, and the convoys were more frequent. The colonel took to doing a round at night not just to see a special man or for a cup of coffee but to speak with the staff and tell us the day's news and – I liked to think – to raise our flagging spirits, for retreat, retreat was still all we heard.

One evening his face was worried. He spoke to each sister and ensured that we had obeyed the latest orders to bring on duty each night not just our tin hat but a small handcase of 'panic' necessities, spare shoes and topcoats.

'You will have no time to go back to your quarters if we decide to evacuate the hospital,' he said firmly, and we knew the news must be really bad.

The men were very quiet as we made our routine rounds but they muttered among themselves, and 'seventy miles from Alex' could be heard in each ward. Several of them asked anxiously, 'Is there any news about getting you girls away?' Bless them, they were always concerned for our safety when things were looking grim.

Rumours flew to and fro. We had all heard the one about tanks being trained on King Farouk's palace, and the British ambassador giving him some ultimatum. Now it was that the sewing-machinists were making Nazi flags openly in the streets of the cities, ready to pull down the Union flag and hoist the swastika instead.

One evening soon after an air-raid alert an enemy plane flew low over the hospital and was heard to crash in the desert behind us. There had previously been warnings of parachutists throughout the Suez and surrounding areas, and as my wards were at the extreme edge of the hospital perimeter I had had the ward broom placed nightly just inside the duty room door of each of my wards, for use as a weapon against an unexpected visitor. That night the orderly medical officer did a round at an unusually early hour. I did not hear his approach until he was opening the door, and I made a grab for my weapon of defence. By the time he had completed his visits to all the wards, his story had reached the length that I had split his skull with my violent attack. All quite untrue, but at least it raised a laugh when humour was in scarce supply.

There was little time for laughing once the battle began. El Alamein – we had heard the men mention the name among a string of others; now it was on everyone's lips.

The medical officers walked through the wards, and any man capable of walking, strong enough to be moved, was discharged or transferred to a Palestine hospital.

Night after night the convoys of wounded came to us by train.

Convoys of ships sailing the ocean spread across sparkling seas, altering course in uniform, are a stirring sight. Not so the convoys of sick and wounded that left the Red Cross train. A line of stretchers coming through the darkness or in the glow of the setting sun, a straggle of bandaged, weary men stumbling behind, tears at your heart.

It was always evening when they came, and the entire staff helped to receive them. Quickly the empty beds would fill – there were never enough, and the men waiting to go to Palestine when the train moved out would be roused to lie on stretchers on the floor down the centre of the ward, or to sit on a chair, and when chairs ran out to huddle on the verandah, their heads on their kitbags.

By how many our correct bed-state of 1,200 patients was increased I doubt anyone really knew. It was no good the ward sister wailing, 'I have no more beds.' The answer was, 'We will put up another tent' – and another eight patients were added to the ward numbers.

With the day staff gone off to their beds, eight night sisters were left to deal with all that the night might bring.

Those were the nights when our midnight meals were uneaten and the primus stoves grew hot with kettles boiling for cups of tea. A quick word here and there as you went up and down the line of wards, in and out of tents, was all you could spare as your eyes searched for the really sick, the man in pain, and the threatened emergency. Among your 200 men and more, there were blood-transfusions running, catheters to be checked, drugs to be given and a rising pulse rate recorded. With all the British orderlies, except a very few, away, the problem of language meant that the POWs and ATS girls replacing them could do little to help with any heavy nursing, however good their intentions.

Those were the mornings when we came off duty more in time for lunch than breakfast. We sat in the mess too tired to eat, too frightened to voice our fears. Had I recorded all those pain-killing drugs, tablets and injections? Had I filled in all the charts? That very sick man: was there anything else I could have done? Had I written enough about him in my report? The patients on the early theatre list: had I got in all their 'pre-med' injections by the right time? And please, God – please, God – grant that I have sent the right patients to the train and not any of the new ones. My worries, my prayers, were in earnest. Unlike my usual regime when on night duty, I slept badly. Just short snatches or restless dreams, when I would wake to worry over what the next night would bring.

Each time on duty the nursing grew more heavy. The very sick men could not be moved on; they would die on the way; so they had to remain; yet every convoy brought more with their own special problems.

As General Montgomery said, 'At Alamein they turned the tide of battle.' Slowly, as the weeks passed, the convoys bringing the wounded grew fewer, the pressure eased, and work returned to normal.

I looked eagerly for mail each day. Eve too had been – and still was – very busy. A postcard whenever the ship was in port was all she managed. Stanley had scribbled a brief note on what must have been the eve of battle; after that I heard no more. One of our sisters was married to an officer in his old unit, and they had had no news, she reported back to me. I missed them both, I realized, now that I had the time and energy to think about things. I could do with a change from this sandy wasteland.

I did not get a change, but I did receive a challenge.

I was back on day duty in the 'jigsaw' ward. I heard the coughing as the stretcher-bearers brought the man to my door. Quickly I glanced at the chart. 'Pneumonia? This is the wrong ward, lads. This is isolation.'

'The MO sent this.' The orderly pulled out a pathological report that read 'Positive swab.'

All eight beds in the 'diph' ward were occupied but fortunately there was an empty room next to them, and I hurried him there.

From the first I did not like his look. He was a very sick man, with the flushed cheeks, shallow breathing, of pneumonia; very different from the composed features of my other 'diph' men. To ease his breathing he would have to be propped high with pillows; to treat his diphtheria he should be lying flat with one thin pillow. One look at his throat and his swollen, thickened neck and I knew we were in for a fight. I had sent my orderly running to the operating theatre with a written request to borrow a tracheotomy set, in case it was needed, before the medical officer appeared and agreed with my gloomy thoughts. He put Fraser (as I shall call him) on the 'Dangerously Ill' list, and he helped me put blocks under the head of the bed in place of extra pillows.

Fraser was a tall, angular man, and he seemed to overflow that narrow army bed as he tossed restlessly. There was no possible way we could keep him in a good position, and when he had very nearly fallen onto the floor, we took the blocks away and propped him up with some pillows.

For a few days he seemed to be winning, his breathing improved, coughing lessened, and then the paralysis began.

The toxin of diphtheria may lead to a form of paralysis when the nerves and muscles are affected. Usually it is only in one or two areas; with Fraser it seemed to be widespread. As he could not swallow, three times a day I passed a tube down his throat, but mixing a liquid diet sufficient to nourish him was not easy, even when supplemented by dried milk and soups from Red Cross parcels. The treatment was worrying for me and frightening for Fraser until he gained confidence, and then he was very fractious with my relief.

His legs and arms were affected, and as we had no physiotherapist in the unit to help, the MO devised some splints. I was at my wit's end trying to prevent pressure sores on this man who could not speak and who had to be lifted and turned frequently. Staff was short at this time, and try as I did, the rest of the patients felt left out and began to talk about 'Sister's pet'.

'Can we risk moving him into the big ward?' I queried when one of the diphtheria patients had been moved out to the tent for convalescence. 'It is two days since he had a tube feed, and he should be able to manage a cup or a spoon for himself.'

The MO thought for a moment before he agreed: 'Yes, it might be a good thing. Make him try to talk and move a little. But as soon as he is free from infection, we must get him down to X-ray. There is something about his chest that I do not like.'

Two days later we found out about that. Dinners had been served and cleared, all patients settled down for an afternoon nap. I was sitting in my office and the orderly away at his meal when shouts and yells came from the diphtheria ward: 'Sister, quick, quick! It is Fraser!'

A heart attack was in my mind, but when I reached him I knew I was wrong. Fighting for air, blue in colour, Fraser was bending forward, a foul stream coming from his mouth and threatening to choke him. Somehow I managed to lift the end of the bed, push a chair under it, turned him on his side, before I shouted to the men, who, all supposed to be lying prone, were sitting up in agitation.

'Bang on your lockers! Shout "Help!" Maybe the next ward will hear.'

It seemed an age before the patients in the next ward, sensing the anxiety in the cries, alerted an orderly, who strolled over saying, 'What's up with you lot?' I sent him running for a medical officer – any medical officer.

'Looks like an abscess has burst somewhere.' That seemed the most likely explanation the MO could give as together we removed the splints that hampered our efforts at dealing with a near-unconscious man. More senior officers came but they had no further treatment to offer until someone remembered that the top brass were visiting another hospital in the area and that one of them was a chest specialist. Later that afternoon he came, but he only shook his head and said, 'There is nothing more you can do. Chap needs an iron lung. There is only one that I know of, and it is in use, in Alexandria.'

Army men look after their own, and they are resourceful. By night time a local unit had made for us ... a *contraption* – that is all I can call it. Except for the hole at one end and a handle sticking out from one side, it resembled a coffin standing on legs. Fraser seemed terrified at the sight of it and clung to my hand as he was lifted in, but he was too ill to resist and once inside seemed to slip into a coma.

The machine was horribly noisy, and we had to organize a gang of men to stand by for manual pumping in case the power failed. Fortunately the room Fraser had had was still empty, so we were able to move him back. I said goodnight to the other 'diph' men, who were unusually quiet after their fright, answered their questions with 'He is still very ill' and went down to a belated dinner in the mess.

The sister in charge of the mess at that time (we had all to take our share of this duty) had once been in charge of the nurses' home of one of London's famous hospitals. Hearing on the grapevine what was happening in my ward, she had waited for me. Most of my colleagues had followed Fraser's illness with interest, as we did when there was a patient who needed so much care, and they had all been pleased when I had reported good progress. This elderly, experienced sister sensed my despair, for she had felt it often enough herself.

'Now, my bird' – we were all her lamb or her bird in moments of distress – 'come along and eat this up. We all know how hard you have worked over that lad. You have done your best; now you must leave him with God.'

And that, I thought, was the end of Fraser.

But no, in three days time he was out of the contraption and after a week joined the other patients again. The men watched over him most carefully, seeming to regard him, as I did, as a minor miracle.

A letter from home telling me that a cousin was coming out to the Middle East coincided with one from her, telling of her arrival.

Dickie was a first cousin, a little older than I, and she had been on the stage since her childhood, mostly in musical comedies. After she married, she and her husband, Ronnie Brandon, ran summer shows on the south and east coasts of England. Now, with a small cast, they had brought their show *Out of the Blue* to join with ENSA's concerts for the troops. They were stationed at our nearest town, and soon I was able to meet them.

Theatrical folk had not often come my way, and after the restrictions of hospital life I found them most amusing and frequently spent my off duty with them whenever our differing spheres of work permitted. And I came to admire the very real efforts they made to entertain and bring some glamour into units, especially the isolated ones. They began to regard my visits as a free clinic, and most of the company sought my advice on cures for insect bites, blistered toes or sandrubbed heels, skin rashes and, of course, gippy tummy. Sometimes I gazed with alarm as one of the company collapsed limply against the side of the truck taking us over rocky roads to some small unit, only to see with amazement an apparently complete recovery when the vehicle stopped and the audience assembled.

It was really something to see how even the young girls

stood up to gruelling journeys over rough terrain. They would sing, dance, act sketches and then walk among a crowd of sweating men in the stifling heat of a tent. They would put over as good a show as the one they gave when they had all the advantages of a theatre.

I was looking forward to entertaining them at my hospital, where they were booked for a show, and had obtained a promise from them to do a few minutes on the verandah of my 'jigsaw' ward, when I received the news that I had been posted to the hospital ship *Oranje*.

7 'Why didn't you write?'

'*Saida, eft el barb.*' Probably my attempt at Arabic was useless but the man at the gate lifted the barrier and we bumped gently over the railway lines to the road beyond. The driver of the transport taking me to the station looked across in surprise.

'Been here long, Sister?'

'Three years,' I answered.

The truck jerked. 'Three years! Here, in this dump? Where are you being sent to next – Siberia?'

'There have been good times and bad.'

Good times – friendship, a sense of unity, of belonging. Days when the battles were going well and the men rejoicing over the news, or when baths and electricity had revolutionized our lives. Days when the heat was not too intense and convoys were few, and the main worry was patients who forgot to refill the water chatties (the earthenware jars that stood on the verandahs) when they had emptied them. And happy times, as when our mess was *en fête* for the marriage of one of our sisters. Bouquets, bagpipes, a horse-drawn carriage and all.

There had been nights when the velvety darkness had wrapped me round like a cloak, the only sound the croak of frogs by the canal. Nights so hectic that they passed in a whirl of activity.

Strange times, when thieves would cut the perimeter wire to let a pack of stray dogs race through the hospital (to be given a wide berth, for fear of rabies). Whilst the *ghaffirs*, our native guards, chased after them with rifles blazing, to the imminent danger of staff and patients alike, the thieves would be deftly removing selected drugs and stores. No doubt they were the same gang who once grazed some camels near the far end of the hospital and then, under cover of darkness, used them to empty the contents of several fully equipped tents.

Patients? They had come in all shapes, sizes and colours, friend and enemy alike. Those who had caused me anxiety were easy to recall; others were more difficult to remember. Some remained a nagging memory, like the small sergeant from Ceylon whose attack of typhoid fever seemed very mild.

'I am going to die, Sister,' he told me.

'Oh no, you are not. Don't be silly. You will soon be well again.'

'It is you who are silly, Sister. I am going to die,' he repeated.

And die he did, though why, neither the medical officer nor I could understand.

One memory would always make me chuckle. A huge African soldier had been brought in one evening from a newly arrived African unit. He was thought to have drunk some poisonous liquid. He spoke not a word of English and seemed to understand only a few basic commands. The medical officer, new out from Britain and unused to foreign troops, waved away my help when I went on duty, and I left him and an orderly preparing to do a stomach-washout; I was busy in the malaria ward. Sometime later I looked across to see the lights still burning, and looked in again. The ward was in chaos, with overturned screens and all patients wide awake. The African, looking surprisingly well, seemed to be resisting all attempts at treatment.

The MO, now sweating profusely, still waved me away, so I went to a surgical ward and borrowed some of the large safety pins used to fasten the bandages of traction patients, and armed also with the largest blanket I could find I went back.

The soldier stared quietly at me as I stood by his bed. He let me wrap the blanket around him. Swiftly I pinned it tight, shouted, 'Sit on his legs!' to the orderly and a nearby patient and got a firm grip on that broad black nose. A gasp, and the tube I had snatched from the MO went down. I left them to the messy job of the washout and went back to my poor malarias. It turned out that there was no poison found, and a very bewildered soldier returned to his unit next day.

The patients in that ward were unusually silent when I did my morning round, until a sergeant asked, 'How come you got that tube down last night when the MO could not manage it?'

'I have the advantage of having nursed sick children,' I told them. 'A toddler cannot always be persuaded to open his mouth or spit out something harmful; you've got to act quickly. I thought a frightened man could be treated like a frightened child.'

There was a roar of laughter from the men, and they stopped looking as if I should have arrived with my broomstick and a black cat.

As the hospital faded into the distance, I knew there was one thing I should never forget – the care of the patients for each other, and for us.

Grumble and grouse as they did when life was calm, their mood changed swiftly when things grew worrying. 'You lasses should not be here.' And their concern was always for the badly wounded, a sick friend – or 'oppo' as the navy calls it. 'Have a look at him first, Sister,' a man on a stretcher would say; 'he's a bit rough,' pointing to another stretcher nearby.

The familiar road was quiet that afternoon, and we soon turned away from the canal towards the villas, the shops of the town, until we reached the railway station. The driver carried my baggage onto the empty platform and wished me luck before he left. There was no one else, it seemed, waiting for the train to Suez.

On the other side of the small station a boy was raiding a pile of wooden crates under the fatherly gaze of a policeman. Tomatoes, eggs and oranges were carefully extracted between the slatted sides and put into a basket. Now and then one went into a separate ragged cloth. When the basket was filled, the cloth was securely tied and handed to the policeman, who received it with a nod and put it beside another that seemed to contain his lunch. Then he watched complaisantly as the boy swung away with his basket.

Law and order? Ah well, such is the way of life in Egypt.

Eleven sisters were on the quayside. I was the last to arrive. We were soon hurried into the waiting launch. Our eyes were turned to the large ship lying apart from a mass of anchored vessels. Against their drab wartime paint, rust-stained and damaged, her white hull gleamed brightly, the broad green band broken at intervals by large red crosses marking her out for all to see as a hospital ship.

Luxury, luxury! That was my first impression as I stepped aboard. The thickly carpeted cabin to which I and another sister were conducted by a steward was large. There were lights – eighteen lights – ringing the mirror, in the wardrobes, above the two beds – beds with sprung mattresses. By the window, a proper window, stood a writing-desk with nearby easy chairs. A tray held glasses and thermos jugs of iced water, and the basin had hot and cold taps. It was all too much for someone from a desert hospital to take in.

After our baggage had been brought in by a small Javanese boy and our much-used and unwanted camp kit taken away for storage, we went to meet the matron, who told us about the ship.

Destined for the Netherlands and East Indies run, the *Oranje* had been on her maiden voyage when the Netherlands were overrun by the Germans, who then declared her a prize of war and ordered her immediate return to the Netherlands. Her captain refused and sailed her to Australia, where she was offered for use as a hospital ship, under Dutch command. Most of her crew, medical and nursing staff remained with her. Many of them had homes and families in the Netherlands or the East Indies and unhappily knew little of how they were faring. Once the ship's nursing sister, our matron had trained in the Netherlands and worked in Britain. She seemed a quiet, competent lady whose English was excellent.

We learnt that we had been brought on board as replacements for an Australian unit who were now serving in the Pacific area. A number of New Zealand sisters and VADs who had been on the ship for two years came and made us welcome. Our British group had come mostly from hospitals in the Middle East, but two had recently travelled out from home and were a source of news about food-rationing and life in wartime Britain. There were a few British orderlies who later joined us, and one very quiet, reserved medical officer who, we were told, was on semi-convalescence following a severe illness.

Matron led us down to what had been the first-class dining saloon, a beautifully decorated place whose main colour was orange; photos of the members of the Royal House of Orange were prominently displayed. On the laden tea-table stood a large dish of fruit. I admired some glossy apples and touched them gently, thinking they were wax, and then I squealed, 'They are real apples!' The girls from Britain looked amazed – they did not know that real crunchy apples were not found in wartime Egypt.

Matron told us that we should be sailing for Durban next day, after the patients had been brought on board; meanwhile she would take us to our wards.

I might have guessed what patients were to be in my charge, for they seemed a part of my war service: I had been allocated eighty patients suffering from tuberculosis. Matron explained that my ward was a completely separate unit, so it was easy to keep isolated, and it was a fine position.

Situated on the top passenger deck facing aft, it had been the ship's nursery and playroom in happier times. Now these two adjoining rooms formed two wards, each housing twenty neat white cots. On either side were glass-enclosed decks where forty hammocks were already rigged for patients who would be up most of the day. There was ample locker space and a good supply of books and games. Behind the wards ran the servery, with a beautifully carved wooden screen depicting a square in Amsterdam. Part of the servery had been made into an office, and when the screen or hatch was bolted up, I had a clear view of the wards and decks. Nothing seemed to have been overlooked: the linen and medicine cupboards were stocked high with supplies, and the diet sheet looked as if any request would be supplied.

My night sister, a former ship's nurse, who came to meet me, told me that her English was not good, but with the aid of a Dutch-English dictionary we would manage.

I learnt that the other hospital ship sailing the same route was of great age and very slow, so that she took nearly three times as long to reach Durban as *Oranje*, who took only eight days. The patients who were considered the most serious would be sent to us.

My cabinmate was about my own age and seemed a cheerful person, and as I snuggled down in bed that night I thought that, whatever tomorrow might bring, this was a very comfortable ship.

The stretcher patients came out from shore on lighters – flat boats used for supplies. Once alongside, they were hoisted up by crane. Two stretchers were placed side by side on a flat pallet, and the New Zealand sergeant major stayed with them. All through the fierce heat of the day he stood astride, balancing the weight and assuring the men of their safety. It was no easy feat, but the loadings went smoothly and without mishap.

It took some hours for my eighty patients to be checked in, but before we sailed in the evening they had all settled down. Some were very ill, two in particular, and I wondered whether they would complete the voyage. Most were very cheerful and convinced that the sunshine of South Africa would provide a cure.

The luxury was extended to them as well as to me. Hospital blues were a thing of the past: white shirts and blue shorts were the rig of the day. There were towels, large, fluffy towels in profusion, and soap wrapped in pink floral paper and supplied in boxes. Boxes! When I had walked the desert at night with a scrap in my pocket with which to cleanse my hands, wash a sick man and catch unwary bugs!

Food was the chief topic among the men. It was the variety and the amount of the servings that amazed them.

I had a hard job persuading the Dutch steward to make helpings smaller, except the ice-cream, which was a firm favourite.

Once we had all settled in, the pace aboard proved very different from that on land. No ebb and flow of patients or sudden emptying of beds to make room for fresh admissions. No off-duty for me either, except for a brief spell after lunch when I could sit in my office to read or write letters. After duty in the evenings we could stroll on deck and chat to officer patients who were still up, or off-duty ship's officers, but always under the watchful eye of our colonel, who, with no recent knowledge of his own teenaged daughters, seemed to feel a great responsibility for us. He had no idea as to whether his family in the East Indies were still alive.

The heat of the Red Sea in summer is fierce. It tried all the patients, and especially my TBs. Their weakened bodies had so little stamina. Each trip there were deaths and burials at sea.

The Dutch required much expression of sorrow at these times. The radio, used to broadcast records and news throughout the ship, would be turned off for the whole day and any arranged entertainment cancelled. The crew, nursing staff and all up-patients were ordered on deck for the service. They stood quietly and respectfully but grumbled about the lack of entertainment for the rest of the day. When this was all repeated next morning, I felt sorry for them. It was hard for men who had served in battle, seen their friends killed beside them, to accept such restrictions. Their grief was too recent, their nerves too strained; they needed distraction, not reminders. I talked to the New Zealand padre and told of the way on British hospital ships, where the service was quiet and attended only by those who wished, so that other sick men were not upset. The padre listened with some concern and spent more time afterwards talking with my patients.

He was a kind man and later in the voyage questioned me when he heard that our salaries were nearly half those of his compatriots. Because it was a Dutch vessel, there were no duty-free concessions for us. We agreed that we

did find it expensive, as in the extreme heat we got
through a lot of fruit drinks (a watchful eye was kept on
anyone drinking alcohol). To our great delight he saw that
a flask of cordial was given to each of us from Red Cross
stores. The New Zealand sisters were well catered for by
their country's Red Cross, who sent to each of them a
large parcel of toiletries, writing-paper, undies or
stockings each month.

There was a difference in the Dutch attitude to nursing.
They cared very well for the patients but stood aghast
when we started on difficult dressings without consulting
the medical officer. These, and regulating blood transfu-
sions etc., should be left to the doctors. But then we
realized they had not yet been used to the pressure of
work with air-raid and battle casualties which had been
with us for so long now.

High up in the isolation of my unit, I was well placed for
enjoying unusual sightings. Apart from glorious vistas of
sea and sky, there would be whales blowing, porpoises
leaping and playing around the ship, and the stealthy
glide or the quick swirl of the triangular fins of sharks.

Eyes other than mine were watching though, constantly. Because *Oranje* had not obeyed the orders to
return to the Netherlands, Germany still issued dire
threats against her, despite our Red Cross status, and
emergency drills were frequent. When patients were
aboard, my lifeboat station was very near my ward, and I
should be very occupied with patients. But if we were
returning empty, I had to go to a boat nearer my cabin,
and there I should be with one Dutch officer, who spoke
little English, and the ship's laundry crew, who were all
Chinese. With shame I admit I did not wish to be
torpedoed at any time but that being with patients seemed
preferable.

We made no stops on the way to Durban, and most of
the men enjoyed the voyage, for the seas were calm. But
my very ill man grew steadily worse. We moved him into a
small cabin near the ward. Nothing was spared that could
be done for him; anything he asked for was produced at
once. The colonel sent him champagne, but I think he

preferred the beer I poured for him. He died peacefully and was buried at sea.

Another man worried me greatly on that first trip, an 18-year-old RAF lad who looked like a frail boy of eleven. Day by day he seemed to slip further away from us. He was looking forward to seeing South Africa, and I feared he would not see it, but he did and gazed around him as his stretcher was carried ashore. Because of his serious condition I was allowed to stay with him and hand him over to the hospital authorities, but despite the care, good food and sunshine they could offer him I did not think he would recover.

It was good to see some of my former patients trooping ashore. They quipped me, 'Where's your hurricane lamp, Sister? Gone soft, have you?'

One of them especially delighted me. He caught my arm as I walked past.

'Forgotten me, have you?' It was his voice I remembered.

'One of the pandas,' I answered.

There had been three of them, all with bad burns to face and hands after parachuting from a burning plane. They had been in the first three beds in one ward, and coming into the darkened hut at night they had looked like pandas as they sat propped up in bed, faces covered in lint except for eye- and mouth-holes, their bandaged hands stretched out before them. They had been a constant worry to me, not because of illness but because the dressings used for their burns were out of supply and instead we were using cod liver oil. The ants were ecstatic; huge armies of them converged on the beds, marching in wide lines across the ward floor or across the ceiling towards the rich smell. The bed legs stood in tins of pure Lysol, a soaked pad placed on top of the mosquito nets, but let one pillow edge or a thin length of string touch a chair, a locker, and those frustrated ants would be climbing up in an instant.

Despite the scars, his face wore a broad smile as I wished him luck and he moved to the waiting ambulance.

Turn-around in Durban completed, we sailed north up the East African coast again. There were a few new faces aboard of special passengers, and we called in at several ports to pick up elderly Italian civilians and wounded Italian prisoners of war whose age, severe illness or wounds would enable them to be repatriated to their own country under a Red Cross exchange. None came to my ward, and I was included in a vast cleaning orgy that Matron organized. (It is true that the Dutch are a very clean nation. QAs did not as a rule find themselves perched on steps washing cabin walls.) As a rest cure she sat us down with piles of linen to repair. There was no hurry, and it was a pleasant change.

One evening, just as we were sailing again from Suez to Durban, I was busy writing up the charts for yet another set of patients.

'A patient from another ward to see you, Sister,' the Dutch steward said.

'Sorry, no visitors here, you know.'

'He says he has the colonel's permission to see you.'

I turned around, and he stood there. Fraser, standing upright as I had never seen him before. He was taller than I had thought, his face more round, and the hand that gripped mine was firm and strong. His voice when he spoke was loud and clear, not the hoarse whisper I had known.

'Fraser! I'm so glad to see you. Are you really well again? Fraser! I can hardly believe it!' And battle-hardened nurse that I was, tears ran down my face.

'There's nothing wrong with me now. They're just sending me down to South Africa for a bit of convalescence.'

'Did that lad come to see you?' the colonel asked on his round next morning. 'I read his notes, very interesting indeed. He is lucky to have pulled through. He gives you credit for that. Yes, a most interesting history.'

'Interesting? You don't know the half of it!' I murmured to myself.

Fraser visited me each day. He told me how the medical officer who had once given him hours to live had seen him again. He had told Fraser to thank the sisters for his recovery and had put forward my name in particular for a 'mention in despatches'. That never materialized, but I didn't care. I had seen Fraser fit and well. I watched him as he left the ship, walking so proudly. I never saw him again, but I hope he survived the war and that peace dealt kindly with him.

The *Oranje* became a very sad ship one day, when news came about the Australian medical unit that had preceded us. They had joined another hospital ship and when sailing empty to pick up patients from battle areas in the Philippines had been torpedoed by the Japanese. No mercy was extended to them, despite the Red Crosses. There was little time to launch boats, and the loss of life was great in shark-filled waters. One sister was known to have survived after a long spell on a raft, her courage and nursing skills enabling her to help those with her. Their loss was mourned by those who had worked with them and enjoyed their company. At the sad memorial service held as we sailed through the sparkling waters of the Indian Ocean, I realized afresh how a regiment, a unit, a ship, becomes a family, its members to be cherished or mourned.

When we were at sea at night, our decks were brightly illuminated, in great contrast to other shipping, where even the glow of a lighted cigarette called down ripe comments from the bridge. Light shone continuously on the green band that circled the ship, on the Red Crosses and the huge flag that we flew. There was no way in which such vessels could be confused with battle or merchant shipping by enemy surface craft.

One evening when I was on deck, a naval launch came past – we were near a port. A rating looked up and called, 'Coo – she looks like bloody Blackpool, don't she?'

On each northbound voyage *Oranje* called at Aden for oil supplies. The whole day was spent there, and sometimes we were allowed ashore. I never repeated my first visit. I thought I had become accustomed to dry heat, but those sunbaked rocks defeated me, and I prayed that I might never be posted to Aden.

Oranje had to be out of Aden before the boom – a netting precaution to prevent submarines (the enemy ones) entering – was put in place before sunset. It was dangerous for *Oranje* to be kept in port overnight, as all lights would have to be switched off for air-raid reasons when she was moored among other shipping. We were all conscious of the anxiety of the captain and crew, and often the ship moved away with only minutes to spare.

Nearing Suez our excitement increased: there would be mail – please God, there would be mail. As soon as the ship was sighted, out came the New Zealand postal launch, to receive a cheer as the bags were hauled aboard, and they brought our mail too. Round sped the postal orderly delivering the precious bundles.

My news from Britain was good. There were a few notes from friends, two postcards from Eve but nothing from Stanley. I was puzzled. I had sent him my new address, and I had written several times and posted them in different ports. I felt I knew him well enough to be sure that, if he had decided to end our friendship, he was too honest a man not to write and tell me. Probably he was like the rest of the Eighth Army, chasing the enemy into North Africa. There would be little time to write. But if he was still working among the minefields of Alamein, why had he not written? I had no means of getting news of him, and my thoughts alternated between the death of an unusually strong friendship and the death of someone rather special.

Remembering that our Dutch colleagues could not enjoy our happiness in getting news of their friends and families, there was an unwritten code of behaviour. Letters were not flaunted openly. We read them in our cabins, in quiet corners, and we shared our news in whispers one to another. The Dutch matron and my night sister always asked politely if the news from home had been good, but realizing the effort it must be for them to enquire, I always kept my answers short and formal.

Suez was packed with shipping when we returned there one very hot day. Quickly the 'buzz' sped through the ship and excitement soared among the New Zealanders: 'We are going home next trip! *Oranje* is going to New Zealand!'

There were no orders awaiting the British unit, and so we

joined in the excitement and began asking questions. I did not like the sound of the Tasman Sea. 'It is shockingly rough,' the New Zealand girls told us. The long, rolling waves that we always met twenty-four hours from Durban had not defeated me. I had kept on duty well enough, but on a diet of dry biscuits, apple and ginger ale. Sea-sickness was considered a weakness by *Oranje* staff. 'Work hard and don't think about it,' was the remedy, they said.

The arrival of a QA matron put an end to our hopes. 'Go to New Zealand? Whatever made you girls think you could go gallivanting off there? You are needed here.'

Ten sisters were posted to the hospital ship *Telemba*, two of us to the hospital carrier *Perak*. My companion was one of those who had joined the *Oranje* soon after leaving Britain, and we were both disappointed at leaving our colleagues, but we were really very fortunate.

Telemba was embarking patients during the invasion of Sicily when she was bombed and sunk within minutes. Many boats put out to the rescue, but patients were lost, sisters injured, and one of them was drowned. She was a quiet, serious woman who had asked to be transferred to a post ashore, as she feared the sea, was a non-swimmer and had had a premonition of death.

As we travelled from Suez to Haifa, where we were to join *Perak*, it was obvious that great preparations for battle were in progress. The road alongside the canal was full of traffic – not just supplies and ambulances but with lorries crammed with men and ammunition. Passing freight trains were loaded with heavy vehicles and tanks. Wherever the invasion was to be, the battles would be fierce.

At Haifa railway station the railway transport officer stared in amazement at our request for transport. 'To the *Perak*? She does not take sisters. A funny old tub that escaped from Singapore. Have a cup of tea and wait whilst I make enquiries.'

He returned a little later to say, 'Yes, they were expecting you but they are doing alterations and your cabin is not ready. You are to be attached to the hospital here for the present. It is a comfortable place. It was known as "the German hospital".'

It was strange to be working in a real hospital again, with spacious, well-equipped wards and airy passages. The pace of life was slow and well ordered, for there were few wounded, and our work was similar to that of any small hospital in Britain: accidents and injuries mainly; only the medical problems differed, with tropical fevers and infections. More hands are always useful, and the staff made us very welcome.

Enquiries about the work of hospital carriers brought the knowledge that they are used to ferry patients from places where a hospital ship could not tie up or anchor. The ship would wait in the vicinity, and the patients then be transferred from the carrier. The work therefore would be to deal with only extremely urgent wounds.

My companion, although recently trained, had little operating experience. I decided I must brush up my very rusty techniques. Although attached to a medical ward, I was allowed to attend the routine operating lists and spent some off-duty hours with a kindly theatre sister, relearning instruments and wartime ways. Theatre work has never taken pride of place for me, but I did my best to acquire more knowledge so that I might bring some degree of efficiency to this new job.

The surgeon, enquiring as to my attendance, took a poor view of my posting. 'Are you a good swimmer?' was his first enquiry, and he went on to suggest that I leave all my heavy baggage in the hospital stores. Thinking of the Australians lost in the Pacific, I was glad that sharks are not a problem in the Med.

There was plenty of off-duty time, and it was strangely pleasant to be able to walk into a town, explore its beauties, old buildings and modern shops and then walk back to the mess. No long, dusty journeys, no planning for a few hours ashore. I found a tailor who made me some slacks, and bought cotton headscarves, which we were allowed to wear in circumstances when uniform dresses and flowing veils would be a hindrance.

The spectacular views from Mount Carmel held a fasci-
nation for me. Looking at the far-off city of Acre bathed in a
sunset glow, I felt nearer to Christ than in any ancient
church. It was on land like this that he had walked, smelt
the herbs and grasses underfoot, and heard the buzzing
bees, the singing birds, that I was hearing. For me there was
serenity on that hillside.

For three weeks we lived and worked in Haifa, and the
time passed peacefully enough, despite the signs of war in
the busy port. Mail came in a few dribs and drabs; most, no
doubt, had gone elsewhere, and still there was nothing
from Stanley, and none of my patients was from the desert
area. There seemed no one to ask for news.

Among my patients, however, was a small group of
Indian Army soldiers. I could not speak with them and had
never before dealt with so many together. Knowing that
their food came from a special cookhouse and thinking to
show my interest, one midday I stirred the container
briskly, extracted a spoonful and nodded my approval, not
realizing until it was explained to me afterwards that my
infidel hands had spoilt it. We live and learn.

Suddenly our orders came: next day we were to report to
the *Perak*.

The morning for me started badly. My uniform trunk,
which had been dropped into shallow water when being
brought ashore at Suez and had seemed unharmed, had
now developed some problem with the locks. A helpful
orderly suggested a strap and padlock. With minutes to
spare and a good taxi-driver, I purchased these and returned in time to say my goodbyes and 'thank you for having
me' before joining my companion already sitting in the hall
surrounded by her baggage. I need not have hurried: we sat
there and waited – and waited. Just before midday a ship's
officer and a rating appeared.

'I'm sorry, ladies, but you are not joining us after all. You
are to return to Egypt. Your train leaves in under an hour.
We shall have to hurry. The railway transport officer has
your orders.'

Egypt again. Where would I be sent this time? Perhaps it
would be Alex? Oh yes, let it be Alex!

My companion had to report to Cairo. I was to go to a hospital on the sandy shores of the Suez Canal. Which explains why, nearing the end of my journey, I sat on that familiar station waiting for a train and watching the same small boy raiding the crates and handing a share to the same fat policeman. Around me the flies and the mosquitoes spread the news to their companions that I was back once more in Canal Zone.

It was like moving to a new class in a school: the surroundings familiar, the classmates unknown. The layout of the hospital was the same, as was my room. With my camp kit set up, mosquito net slung, shabby curtains unpacked but not yet ironed, I could be back a few months in time. At least here there was plenty of electricity, as we were beside a large prisoner of war camp which was ringed by lights.

Comfortable beds, luxury bathrooms were things of the past. I was back with the sand and the flies and those fat crickets that persist in climbing walls and ceilings so that they can fall with a squashy plop into a precious cup of tea or onto the fresh page of a report book.

The hospital was busy, but not with wounded. These were men arriving from Britain or other areas whom illness or accident had struck, and the POW camp supplied us with patients as well as orderlies.

Unlike my former desert hospital, a high matting fence surrounded the sisters' quarters. Indian troops supplied our guards. Goodnights to husbands, boyfriends and anyone else had to be said well away from the entrance gate, or the stern reprimand 'For memsahibs only, Sahib,' would be spoken firmly as the guard moved forward to restrain any male intruder.

My cousin and her company soon made contact with me, and I enlisted their help in getting news of Stanley, whom they had met and liked. They were still entertaining troops in the area of his previous camp, but nothing came of their enquiries. I asked patients in similar units for news of him, but none had been up in the battle zones. Sometimes, when on a shopping trip to town, I bumped into old friends, but the desert road to Cairo was a different one which did not touch my old hospital. I missed Stanley, as well as other friends.

I was working chiefly on relief duties, a dull job often given to newcomers. 'You will get used to the wards best by moving around them' is the excuse; in reality it is because 'We want to know what you are good for.' The constant changes, a few hours here, a day or so there, give little chance of getting to know the patients. I was always glad when a familiar face popped up – someone with a recurrent attack of malaria or a man prone to dysentery with yet another spell in hospital. They greeted me, and we exchanged news of different places, better or worse, and of people we had met.

Some of them I remembered as 'good', others as 'difficult' patients, for there are times when such a man can cheer or disturb a whole ward. There are other times when patients can make you sick and weary with their persistent grumblings, and more when they make you feel a cherished member of a close family.

It was a time like this when I went, early one evening, in answer to a message from an orderly. The ward sister was off duty, and one of the men with a badly wounded leg was in pain. The dressings on a huge, gaping wound had been disturbed and needed to be renewed. Screens were put in place, and I started on what proved a long and painful process. When I had nearly finished, I looked over the screen and said, 'Will someone get a mug of tea for this lad? I have given him a rough time.'

A group of men sitting on their beds – we had few chairs in the wards – looked at me with interest, though why I did not know, and a sergeant whom I had seen before came forward and asked me abruptly, 'You ready to get back to your own wards now, Sister? Me and the orderly will see everything is all set for the night. You get along now.'

Relief sister or not, I don't take orders in my wards, I thought. These men who stayed a long time in the same hospital were always a nuisance and thought they could take over the whole place. I made a few enquiries as to the health of some of the others and left to a sudden flurry of good wishes. Strange, I thought, and wondered what had got into them.

The orderly of the ward in which I had been working seemed to be hovering as if waiting for me.

'Something wrong?' I asked.

'No, oh no – they are all fine, just fine' and with a smile almost splitting his usually dour face he flung open the duty-room door.

There stood Stanley. He was very pale, very thin, and limped as he walked towards me, but the warmth of his welcome was evident.

'Why didn't you write?' We said the words in unison, and followed them with, 'I did! I did!' And then I asked, 'What has been wrong? You are limping – have you been wounded?' He nodded, then turned me towards the light.

'Let me see what these months have done to you. I heard you had left the *Oranje*, gone to the *Telemba*, and then I heard she had gone down.'

My orderly, still beaming, brought in a tray of tea and announced, 'Night Sister is on her way down.'

A few minutes later she came in, far earlier than usual, for the busy wards are always the first call.

'Everyone well? Have you finished the report? Good. I shall read it later. Give me the drug keys, and get off.'

I poured the tea when she had gone. 'The grapevine is working overtime,' I laughed. 'I didn't think anyone here knew about you.'

'I contacted your cousin Dickie, found out where you were, smiled at your mess sister and then tipped off your orderly to get you back here. I did not want to surprise you in the middle of a ward.'

'Bless them!' I said and thought how the warmth and closeness of a unit can embrace you in times of joy as well as in sorrow.

It took a long time to tell all that had happened to us in the past few months. No doubt some of Stanley's letters would journey to New Zealand and back, and reach Palestine, before I received them. And those I had written could do a round of the hospitals in Alexandria – if they had not been destroyed by bombs previously – until they reached Cairo, where Stanley was on light duty until his limp improved. Meanwhile he was on a few days' sick leave and staying at the same hotel as my cousin and her company.

Over the next week my off-duty was spent swimming and lazing in the pleasant gardens of the French Club whilst we talked of our travels.

At first Stanley told me only of his time in the hospitals in Alexandria to which he had been taken. He had refused treatment for a wound in his leg, thinking it only slight, but he had finally had to give in when walking became impossible. Then one evening he suddenly broke into a long account of the battle of El Alamein, telling me what I had heard from other men of the incredible noise of the bombardment with which the battle started. He went on to tell of his admiration for Montgomery's planning, of the white-taped tracks which had guided the men and tanks, and how the military policemen had stood at junctions directing the battle traffic as if they were on duty in a town on market day, oblivious to the rain of shells around them. He had great admiration too for the Quaker unit which worked among the stretcher-bearers and the ambulances. He did not speak of the battle again for a long time. It was as if a bubble had come to the surface of his mind, burst and gone.

Of his work in the minefields after the war had moved on into North Africa he said very little. With only a small number of men, he had spent his time extracting guns and vehicles from these dangerous spots, watching for the ever-present booby-traps and burying the dead found still lying there. Many miles were traversed seeking vehicles spotted from the air or known to be in certain places. Because of this, their rations and more often their water supplies had been very sparse, and looking at him I could see the toll these arid places had claimed.

Soon he went back to Cairo, his limp almost gone. My cousin had moved westward and was expecting soon to finish her tour in North Africa and then return home. She had promised to contact my family as soon as she arrived and tell them of our meetings. For a while my busy social spell seemed to have come to an end.

Then I had a letter from Stanley, saying he was not going back 'into the blue' but was leaving Cairo for a workshop in the Sinai Desert. Sinai? Surely that was the range of hills we could see from the high ground behind the hospital. He would be quite near – except that the Suez Canal divided our units.

Near Suez there was a pontoon bridge by which army transport crossed, most helpful when working but, because of precautions against enemy submarines, the times when it was in position were constantly being altered, and of course neither it nor the anti-submarine net could be used when a convoy of ships was entering or leaving the canal. That bridge regulated our meetings. We were completely subject to its vagaries. Arrangements of off-duty, messages sent by letter, by ambulance and lorry-drivers, even by passing despatch riders all came to naught if the bridge was not in operation.

But we did manage it sometimes, and it was on a night when the moon was bright and silvery stars hung as if by threads from a violet sky that I promised to marry Stanley. There can be few women so privileged as to remember a time such as that, when palm trees rustled in a candle-lit garden and the fragrance of night-scented blossom hung in the quiet air.

An elderly departmental sister came to give me her best wishes next morning. 'I am very happy for you,' she said, 'very happy. Somehow I had thought that you would spend the rest of your life in nursing, in the tropics.'

'Maybe I shall,' I answered. 'Marrying a regular soldier – maybe I shall.'

How strange that she had guessed what I had only recently decided for myself – that this was where I would work when the war was over. The poverty I had seen, the need for skilled care in these lands, once unknown to me and now so familiar, pleaded for my help. Now I had altered those plans – and when would the war be over? The euphoria that had gripped us all after El Alamein had faded. Advances in Italy were slow, the invasion of Europe from Britain would come one day – the troops were forever telling us that – but whenever it came, the cost would be high. Yet we began to plan useful gifts that would survive the rough handling of our baggage and fit into our already bulging trunks on the journey home.

The weeks passed; my meetings with Stanley grew fewer, as he was spending little time with his unit. Special courses were being arranged for work in 'Recovery'; he was involved with this and was often away in Cairo. Then he sent me a message to meet him there.

On my next day off I set out early in the morning. He was awaiting my arrival, and once I had washed off the dust of the journey we started a day of celebration. First into Cicurel's, the big French store, to buy a birthday gift for his mother, to whom he was greatly attached. We added a prayer for its safe arrival. How many pairs of stockings, slips and nighties had I chosen for men's nearest and dearest, and how few seemed to have reached their destination, with the hazards of the Egyptian postal service, enemy action and customs?

Stanley had to spend part of the day at a meeting. This gave me a chance to visit the hairdresser, without which appointment no trip to Cairo was complete. We met again for tea at Groppi's, and then as darkness fell we made our way to the Street of the Jewellers. Like two children let out of school, we moved from shop to shop until, having made the choice, we ran back to the first we had entered and bought *the ring*. That memory still lies tight inside the gold and sapphire circle.

The Pyramids, like Luxor, are said by wise men to look their best by moonlight. They were certainly looking well as we walked around them that night, and a passing string of camels turned them into a perfect picture postcard. There was time for a leisurely dinner at the nearby Mena House before we started back across the sandy road to our units.

The weeks passed and then one evening a POW burst into the ward in which I was working and screamed a spate of Italian to a compatriot, who, dropping the clean blue kit he had just brought from the store into an untidy heap on the floor, burst into loud sobs. The pair of them ran from the ward to join a stream of POWs hurrying towards the fence.

'Now,' said my patients almost in unison, 'now perhaps they will believe what we have been telling them all day.'

Escorted by destroyers, southwards down the canal sailed Italian ships of war. Their colours were no longer flying, for Italy had surrendered.

8   The Home Front

Marriage in Egypt, we had decided after long discussions, was not for us. Several of our friends' weddings had been celebrated there and had later broken down. We decided to wait until our return to Britain. Our two names were already listed with those whose overseas service had lasted four years or more, and although we could not hope to sail home together, we believed that the separation would not be for long.

I was the first to receive my orders. I was to report to Heliopolis, to the place where my duties in Egypt had first started. The hotel had long since been taken over for a hospital. Now it was being disbanded, all patients had been discharged and the equipment and stores packed, ready for the return to Britain. The accompanying sisters would be made up from many units.

There was not a room for me in the sisters' quarters, so with another sister I was given a room on the ground floor near the now empty kitchen. Our camp beds were erected and our mosquito nets slung from the beams.

During my first night in this room I awoke to a faint 'scratchy' sound. A mouse? A rat? No ... the noise was quieter than either would make. Also I sensed 'movement'. I felt under my pillow for my torch, switched it on and screamed! My companion sister woke and screamed as well. I guess we could almost have been heard in Alex! Our eyes were glued to the beams, from which hung our two mosquito nets, now covered with a swaying mass of cockroaches.

Footsteps pounded along the corridor. 'In here!' I shouted as loudly as I could. 'Switch on the light!'

Army boots were crunching more of the creatures carpeting the floor as the sentry burst in. The sergeant of the guard and his men shook the nets free of the vermin and spread a thick ring of insect powder around our beds. Then two large mugs of tea were made for us.

'There's plenty of sugar in them,' the sergeant said, 'for you two ladies have had a nasty shock.'

Next morning a sympathetic colleague cleared a space for me in her bedroom, well away from the kitchens, and my companion too was offered alternative hospitality.

Two days later, while we were under the 'four hours notice to move', I awoke with a splitting headache and a rising temperature. The MO who visited me was an old friend who had seen me with malaria before.

'Another attack?' he queried. I shook my head – very carefully.

'No ... I don't feel the same. This is a different headache, and my eyes are aching.'

'Sandfly fever, most probably,' he suggested. Malaria meant two or three weeks in hospital, whereas sandfly fever could be over in a few days. At this stage, who would want to lose the chance of going home? I pleaded, gently but sincerely, against being sent to hospital.

The MO whispered to me very quietly, 'I don't think we are moving for forty-eight hours. Do you think you can make it up that gangway then?' More loudly he said, 'Sandfly fever, usual treatment. Rest here quietly and I will come and see you if we get sudden orders to move.'

He was quite right. It was two days before we left.

My recollections of the journey to Alexandria are vague. People were kind; they saw that my camp kit and heavy baggage were collected and packed my hand luggage, but after that, loaded with small cases, hung about with gas masks and capes, tin hats and the collection of papers without which no one could board the ship, there were no spare hands to help me. I stumbled along in their wake, my head still ringing, made better or worse by the quinine, aspirin and other infallible remedies pressed upon me. The thought of a comfortable berth similar to that on the *Oranje* kept me going.

I was doomed to disappointment. The ship, of some unknown origin, now pressed into service as a troop ship, was incredibly crowded. I found myself in a cabin originally intended for four persons, now to hold twelve. Mine was the top bunk of a tier of three. There was a bathroom, but as part had been taken off to make room for extra berths, some rather large sisters were apt to trap themselves behind the door and squeal in panic as they struggled to get out. There were no drawers or wardrobes and not even sufficient hooks for us to have one apiece. My topcoat served as a pillow throughout the journey and was never the same again.

Where to stack our cases was a problem, as the floor was needed for feet, not luggage. My case was hauled up to the end of my bunk and secured with a rope. For once I was glad of my lack of inches, as there was no way even I could stretch out. Throughout the journey, rough nights were enlivened by cases, tin hats and such crashing down, to roll around and strew their contents in all directions.

We queued for everything – for a bath, the loo and meals. These were served cafeteria-fashion in a surly take-it-or-leave-it fashion. Space on deck was for standing only; chairs were seldom to be seen. Most of the voyage I spent on my bunk.

There was none of the joyous anticipation that I had expected to feel at this long-awaited time. It was now more a question of survival to ensure that home was reached. Reading and sleeping seemed the best way of passing the time. Rest at night was difficult. There were always some who came in late and crept in carefully in darkness, only to fall over stray objects lying around. This without fail woke up some who had gone to sleep earlier; these then got up and caused the bathroom plumbing to start a unique concert of shrill whistles alternating with resounding thumps. Sometimes this cacophony could be silenced by further flushing; at other times nothing would prove effective, and with ears covered we would have to endure its complete repertoire.

Boat drills did little to cheer me. The exit from the cabin was up a narrow, rickety staircase with a twist in the middle. One large or injured lady could block it completely. A hundred sisters take up rather a lot of room, and most of us were allocated to this exit. Proceeding swiftly but calmly as instructed, with life-jackets on, some rather larger sisters would find it impossible to turn the corner; and with a further 300 men aiming for the next staircase, our chances looked rather slim in a torpedo attack.

When we tied up at a Scottish port, we sat all afternoon and evening awaiting the call 'Nursing officers will now disembark.' When it did come, by some strange chance I led the way down to the lower deck where the gangway was situated, but when I got there, I found I was too short to step over the ship's side onto the gangway. For an instant a light was flashed onto me, and then over the tannoy came an irate voice: 'Will the nursing officers disembark *now*?' There were a few moments of confusion until a sturdy block of wood was produced – and we were on home soil.

The dockside railway tracks were covered in snow, but the waiting train was warm. A smiling woman – yes, even at 1 a.m. she was smiling – gave us each a packet of sandwiches and pies. Along the carriages, the message was passed: 'Settle yourselves as comfortably as you can. There are no changes until we reach our destination.' London, I thought complacently, and swathed my hair in a scarf, took off my shoes, put on some slippers and, hardened travellers that we were, we were all soon asleep.

A loud call suddenly awoke us: 'All nursing officers out! Hurry, please. Your train is waiting.'

7 a.m. at Crewe, and 100 sisters ran in a motley stream along the platform, over the bridge, along another platform. Scarved, slippered, draped in travelling-rugs, grabbing, dropping and regrabbing an overspill of hand luggage, tin hats clattering as they rolled around us, we boarded the other train. Some had their hair in plaits, some in rollers and well ... what did it matter? We were going *home*! Home to meet our families, our boyfriends, our nearest and dearest. *Now*!

But we were anticipating too soon, for those reunions were still some days away.

We spent quite a time waiting in sidings. And then that

afternoon Abergele welcomed us. On the platform stood trestle tables, and we were offered and drank hot tea or soup. We ate buttered scones as we waited to be billeted. Then we were led away to more lorries or on foot to various houses.

Someone had given a great deal of time and thought to ensure that we had a warm reception. Every house had been granted extra fuel, blankets and hot water bottles. Someone had obviously realized the contrast between the heat of Egypt and the winter cold of Britain. With several others I was sent to a pleasant guest house. It was very comfortable, our sitting-room warm, and the good Welsh cooking very acceptable.

The real frustration was the delay with our baggage. No one had explained to the stationmaster the amount of luggage that one hundred sisters returning from overseas would bring. One lorry was sent to the station to collect it, and storage arranged in a small cottage in the town, as distribution to so many billets was impossible. By next day the cottage had been completely filled, including the toilet, passage and stairs, and the railway vans were not yet emptied. Another house and part of a hall were used, and still some trunks remained at the station. No travel warrants were to be issued until all baggage had been claimed.

There was no logical way in which to set about tracing our belongings. Trunks, valises, blanket bundles and kitbags were piled indiscriminately between the four places. To reach the bedrooms in the cottages was almost impossible, for the luggage blocking the stairs. We hurried from them to the hall and up to the station, trying to recognize a mark, a label, among the stains and scars of our much-travelled cases; not an easy task, as so many of them had come originally from the same stores. Often when someone gave a cry of joy the object of their attention was buried too deep beneath the pile or was too heavy for us to extricate it.

Finally some troops were sent to ease the situation.

Having traced it, pulled it out onto a vacant space on the nearest pavement, came a further problem – how to get a trunk, valise and kitbag to the railway station? The townsfolk came yet again to our aid with handcarts and wheelbarrows when cars and lorries had to give up for lack of petrol.

No doubt the stationmaster and the postmaster of that town remembered our arrival for many years because of that mountain of luggage and the rush of telegrams and letters caused by the delay.

It was early evening when I reached London and set out on the last lap of the journey to my parents' home on the edge of Kent. Because of bomb damage, traffic was diverted to a station strange to me. It was a dark night, with flurries of snow, and the stations were unnamed. After several stops I enquired of my fellow passengers our whereabouts. No one answered. I asked again before I remembered that 'Careless talk costs lives.' Meekly I apologized, saying I had just returned from overseas. Someone inspected me by torchlight and then told me the number of stops to my destination.

Once there, again there was the problem of baggage. A taxi was unheard-of, it seemed. With my help the weary porter stacked it in the corner of the booking-office for the night.

I walked home through dark, snow-slushy streets to find that my parents, thinking it too late for me to arrive that night, had already gone to bed.

Christmas was spent in a round of quiet celebrations. All the family assured me that they were well, yet I saw a weariness widespread among them. Like the city of London itself, they seemed battered in body but not in spirit.

My aunt came from Sussex, and as I stood waiting for her at Victoria Station, her dog recognized me. Yelping wildly, he rushed forward, his leash flying loose and striking at and tripping up unwary passengers. He caused a commotion and so many apologies that my aunt and I forgot to greet each other.

There was much to learn of wartime Britain. To understand the problems of wartime rationing of food and clothing. The shortage of fuel and electricity was, I think, the worst problem for those of us who returned in wintertime. We missed the heat and shivered in the meagre warmth of small coal fires and one-bar gas and electric ones.

My next hospital, on the Welsh border, was yet another unusual one. Now I was to be working 'behind the wire' in a prisoner-of-war camp in which severely wounded or very sick, often terminally ill, Italians and Germans awaited repatriation through the Red Cross efforts. There were only eight sisters, most of whom were in low medical categories and needed a quiet post.

The work was very easy indeed, mostly supervision of medicines and drugs, diets and sometimes dressings, but often these were done by their own orderlies under our watchful eyes.

The two nationalities had separate wards, and even at night they were distinctive: the Germans, well ventilated and extremely tidy; the Italians, stuffy and slovenly. The wards were in the care of their own physicians or surgeons but supervised by a British medical officer. Surgery could be undertaken by them, but the operating theatre was in the charge of a QA sister, and no operations could be performed unless a British surgeon was present. Most of the surgical patients had had one or more limbs amputated months or years earlier and needed little attention from me. Some of the medical men were very sick, and it was in these wards that most of my time was spent.

The difference between the two nationalities was very obvious when I went into a ward. The Germans would stop speaking and move towards their beds as soon as the British orderly and I walked in, any noise whilst we were there calling forth a reprimand from their sergeant. The Italians would continue to amble about, chattering as they went, in an effort to pretend to ignore us, until the British orderly shouted 'Stand to your beds!', which slowly they would obey, only to continue their daily grumbling about 'Potatoes – every day potatoes – why no spaghetti?'

The pace of life was slower here than that I had known,

but there were many changes, many adjustments I needed to make, especially about the American troops flooding into the area. White or coloured, their behaviour amazed me. No where else had troops whistled at me as they passed along the road by the hospital; and remarks were called, despite the lieutenant pips obvious on my shoulders. I felt sad too for the British troops sitting in the cheap seats at the cinema whilst the GIs swaggered to the best seats accompanied by the local girls. I felt like calling out to these women, 'Your men have been fighting for you in Greece, Egypt and God knows where. Can you not give them some of your company?' I could not forget those nights when I had listened to so many stories from men far from home, worried sick over the fate of their loved ones.

But it was one evening when I went into the town that I was really shocked. A sister whom I had worked with overseas was joining the unit, and I thought I would welcome her at the station as I was off duty that evening. If I was there to help with her baggage, we might manage to get back in time for dinner. The light was dim but not really dark as I walked towards an arched passageway near the station. A policeman standing near called, 'Just a moment, ma'am, and I will walk through with you.'

I was surprised by his offer and laughed as I replied, 'Thank you very much but don't bother.'

'Just wait, please, Sister.' He finished speaking to a man and hurried across to me. 'New here, are you?' he asked. 'This is not a good spot for you sisters or any women to walk through alone' – he glared at some troops lounging nearby – 'not these days.'

'It is kind of you,' I laughed again, 'but I've been walking around hospitals overseas since this lot started.'

'Maybe.' He pointed out my route once we had rejoined a main street, and turned back.

It did not seem right to me – not in my own country, in Britain – that I needed to be escorted.

My mother wrote that the raids were getting very bad again in London. When Stanley came home, she thought we should arrange a quiet wedding, as it would be wrong to bring his family down from the North. It was plain from her letters that she and my father were spending most nights in the Anderson shelter in the garden; nearby houses had been hit, and there were casualties.

Stanley's letters spoke of increasing hopes for a quick return, and I waited expectantly for a cable telling me he was on his way. I spent my next days off in Sussex making tentative plans for a wedding ceremony in the small village church I had often attended. Would it be wise to have guests come to Sussex?

I was concerned about my aunt's health, for to me there seemed a great deterioration in her medical condition. I worried about her being alone (her maid had gone off to work in munitions), but when I telephoned my cousins I could tell they thought I was fussing as I had seen her only once before since my return to Britain.

Two days later I was busy in the British ward which was 'outside the wire', dealing with two young soldiers who had suffered a strangely similar accident. 'I walked into the barrack-room door in the blackout, Sister.' Both needed treatment for swollen eyes and bruised knuckles. The sergeant major came into the ward and told me that the colonel wanted me – immediately. Another move, I thought, as I put on my cuffs and went to his office. Matron was there as well.

'Bad news I am afraid, Sister. You are needed in Bexhill. I have no further information. If you hurry, there is a London train you might catch.'

Transport had been arranged, and Matron pushed a pack of sandwiches into my hand. With a small bag of hastily snatched-up clothes I was soon on my way.

I had heard no radio news that morning, and I was surprised when the stationmaster said, 'Not going to a very good spot for leave, are you? Shocking raid they had there on the coast last night. You will have some delays, I expect.' My face must have given me away, for he was very kind and came back after a few minutes to tell me that he had telephoned the next stop to find out if a fast London express would be stopping to take on water, as it sometimes did, and would the railway staff get me aboard, which explains how I came to be taken off the platform and pulled up into the train by some hefty soldiers.

Until then I had not thought that my aunt might have been injured or killed by enemy action, but everyone looked at me questioningly when I said I was in a hurry to get to Bexhill. The news of the raid seemed widespread.

It was nearly midnight when, by devious routes and delays, I at last walked along the well-known lane to my aunt's house. In the darkness it seemed to be standing unharmed, although I had passed through some severe damage. There was no sign of life until my cousins woke up. They had decided I had not been granted leave and had gone to bed.

My aunt was dead, but not directly because of the raid. After the 'All Clear' had sounded, she had gone back to bed and seemed to have died peacefully in her sleep.

There was much to do in the short space of time we could spend there; both my cousins were in senior posts in essential work. The vet came, quietly to put to sleep one very elderly dog and several aged cats. Personal papers were sent to the solicitors, and the house was straightened and securely locked before we travelled to London for her burial beside her husband.

Another page in my life had turned, and my wedding plans altered yet again.

A quiet place in nursing was never mine for long. Soon I was off to Dorset. The gathering of troops massing for the Second Front – words on everyone's lips now – increased all the way as I got nearer to the south. From the train I looked onto fields thick with soldiers and vehicles. Tanks lumbered along roads where only cows had ambled to and from the meadows and milking-parlours. Military policemen stood on village greens or road junctions, directing military convoys. I had seen it all before, but not to this extent – no, nothing as big as this.

My guardian angel must have remembered me again, for the town near the hospital was the family home of my great friend from my early days in the children's wards. She had worked and was still working in the training school in which we had taken our general nursing, but her parents remembered my visits from pre-war days and welcomed me into their family circle as warmly as when we first met. Their sitting-room was a haven of rest from the bustle of the hospital, their garden a delight in which to sit and admire its beauty or wander around, trowel or secateurs in hand, trying to remember former gardening skills. That happy home was a real bonus for me.

Mary's mother bubbled with excitement over my coming marriage. Why not be married in their church? All the family had attended there for generations. 'And Mary will be my bridesmaid!' I sighed contentedly. I went to the hotel nearby to look at wartime menus for wedding receptions.

How many plans for weddings were made in wartime, only to be altered again and again? The hopes of today become the fears of tomorrow.

The hospital seemed more like a transit camp for nursing staff than anywhere else I had known. Young nurses just joining and awaiting their first units came; others being briefed for specialized work in the coming campaign lived in the mess for a few nights; a few back from overseas waited for their disembarkation leave to be awarded before they set off for home. At times the mess was so crowded there was little space to move; at others the dining-tables were almost empty, and we were looking after several wards. I could have four orderlies and two extra sisters with me in the morning and by night-time be struggling along with only one harassed VAD.

One of the regular QAs in the unit had been my senior in my training days. It was good to meet up with her again. Suddenly she was posted away, and later we had sad news of her. She had been in the hospital ship *Amsterdam* when it was sunk in the Channel. With another sister, both strong swimmers, she had ferried wounded men to the rescuing boats. Swimming back yet again to the sinking vessel, they were trapped and drowned as the ship went down. Seventy-five men are said to have been saved by their heroic efforts.

When she left the unit I was given her ward, the

officers' hospital. As is customary, it was a mixture of wards and rooms for medical and surgical patients. Another 'jigsaw' ward but with a difference. These were officer patients, some of whom were very conscious of their rank. Officers' wards are always difficult to run; with staff in a constant state of ebb and flow, it was very difficult indeed.

Senior officers seemed to be still nurturing peacetime ideas, objected to sharing a room, being in a ward. One demanded to know why a young lieutenant had been given a room, whilst he, of senior rank, was put with two other patients? Annoyed, I snapped back, 'If you had lost both legs, I am sure he would be glad to have you as a companion.' A colonel came uninvited into my office and sat down to telephone without a word to me. When I enquired about this, he said he wished to ensure that his wife, who would be visiting him, had a quiet room at the hotel, but a better idea would be if I went and inspected it, and would I do so that evening, so that he could ring her before bedtime? After the comradeship I had seen in the army in the desert, even in the most senior officers, I found this attitude very hard to understand.

Medical officers came and went, like the rest of the staff, each of them with his own likes and dislikes, his own pet treatments which were altered again and again. Some of my poor orthopaedic patients alternated between splint, plasters and exercise almost daily, until we were all bewildered.

My life would have been much harder if it had not been for two VADs. One was a cousin of Her Majesty The Queen; the other, much younger, the daughter of a wealthy brewery family. Nothing daunted them. They charmed the men, laughed when all seemed chaos, and did, without a murmur, any skilled or menial task that had to be done. It was my first experience of working with VADs, and I honoured them.

One morning I went on duty to find no staff in the ward kitchen and the breakfast tins there.

'Your orderlies have all gone, Sister. Can I pour the tea or something?' a young officer enquired helpfully.

From the bathrooms came the sound of scrubbing. There were my two VADs, one wielding a lavatory brush and cleaning-powder, the other scrubbing toilet floors.

'Morning, Sister,' one called cheerfully. 'We're almost finished here. Have the breakfasts arrived? Good, we'll be on to those in a jiffy. Isn't it a lovely morning?'

I was willing to bet that the cleaning of lavatories had not been on the curriculum at Roedean or whichever expensive school they had attended.

The talk was all of the Invasion now. When and where would it be? Suddenly all leave was cancelled, and I still had no news of Stanley's arrival.

Over our heads, one fine June evening, the bombers began to roar. Wave after wave of them flew past. Up-patients ran from the wards to stand in the roadway, shouting and waving, and we followed them. It was the evening of 5 June, and with those bombers we knew that the Invasion had begun.

The chaplain stopped beside me. He glanced at me, at the African Star pinned to my cape and, ignoring the tears in my eyes, said quietly, 'Pass the word, Sister. The chapel is open, will remain open all night for private prayer. We owe them that at least.'

Later I knelt there, but the prayers I wanted to say did not come. I was remembering a boy of eighteen who lay on the verandah of that desert hospital, the reek from his burned legs too strong to have him in the ward. I recalled his screams if I did not get to him with an injection that would send him to sleep before the noise of the bombers leaving a nearby airfield sent his tormented mind winging back to that burning tank in which he had been trapped. The day staff thought me soft for sedating him, but then they never heard those screams, tried to hold those flailing arms.

Although we had emptied the wards in readiness, the battle casualties did not come to us; instead we were used for routine accident and sickness patients who kept us busy.

And then the cable for which I was waiting arrived. Stanley was on his way home. It was followed fairly quickly by another: 'I am here.'

All leave was cancelled still. Now travel was restricted. I could not get away. My hopes of a wedding – anywhere – faded daily.

The matron had listened to my request and had given me her best wishes before she shook her head sadly. The colonel took my hand, wished me good luck and tore up my application form for leave in front of me. The chaplain, smiling his sympathy, came to the ward to tell me his appeal on my behalf had failed.

On the telephone Stanley listened, told me not to worry. He still loved me. Just leave it all to him.

To whom he spoke I have no idea, perhaps being a regular he knew the right strings to pull, but the day after I received a telegram from him saying, 'Arrangements being made for wedding here.'

The colonel sent for me. Again he shook my hand and repeated his good wishes, and then like a magician he waved before my delighted eyes a leave pass.

Very early next morning I was on my way to Newcastle-on-Tyne, the local post office overloaded with telegrams telling my family of my plans. In my case was my wedding outfit: a pale blue dress and camelhair coat. Also in my case were two bottles of whisky – which had caused much laughter ...

Officers were allowed to purchase through their mess a limited supply of alcohol. Never having had much interest in this before, I had, since realizing the scarcity of it in Britain, determined to take up my issue to help with the wedding festivities. On approaching the mess sister, I had been told that, 'In this unit sisters don't have an issue.' Mystified, I made further enquiries and discovered that it was the practice to transfer it to the medical officers' mess. I let this be known to other sisters who had recently joined, and we voiced our objections in no uncertain manner and the procedure was reversed. We were not popular with mess sister or the medical officers; in fact, I was almost accused of being an alcoholic. But the joke really came when the hastily wrapped parcel, a wedding gift, given to me on behalf of our mess, turned out to contain a bottle of whisky. Stationery at that time was in very short supply, and I did appreciate the effort someone must have made to cycle into town and search for a suitable card, which, with 'Birthday' scratched out and 'Wedding' substituted, was tied to the bottle.

The journey to my wedding was not uneventful. A buzz bomb hit the railway station as my train pulled into London. With the other passengers, I lay flat on the platform as glass showered around us. I was taken to the 'Ladies', where I sat shocked and crying, not from fear or injury but because my new, expensive uniform coat was stained with thick oil.

'Look at it!' I wailed as an elderly attendant brushed glass from my hair. 'Look at it, and I am going to my wedding!'

'Never mind, ducks. You are still alive to get there. That's summat, ain't it? Give me your coat. There is something the engine-drivers use might clean it.'

Whatever it was, the result was not perfect, but I was grateful.

My father, who, unbeknown to me, had come to the station in the hope of meeting me and had been searching among the injured, found me. He said Mother could not face the long journey north, and he could not leave her alone with such raids as they had been having recently. We had a few brief moments together and then hurried to the next station, another of the buzz bombs coming down near us as we travelled. The train for Newcastle was already waiting. I kissed my father, gave him a hug and ran to the barrier as he turned away.

'Best wait for the next,' the ticket-collector said. 'Train's packed.'

I waved my first-class warrant at him, and the guard, whistle in hand, opened a door and pushed me in.

A ticket for a canary in a cage would have been as much use. I could not move down the corridor, which was jammed with soldiers and their kitbags. The handle of the door was digging painfully into me with every jolt of the train until a sergeant standing in the toilet doorway eased back an inch or so, and with him and three other soldiers, that is where I stood for the rest of the journey. Being 'packed like sardines' is an under-statement – sardines had it cushy compared to us. There were stops where no one could get in, stops in sidings because of raids and damage. The afternoon wore on, and still the journey did not end. I had sandwiches and an apple in my case, but although it was heavy on my feet, there was no way I could lift it up, let alone open it. Some men got out at Darlington but others crowded in.

At Newcastle, getting out was a nightmare. Our cramped, sore feet could scarcely move. Stanley was there waiting, that much I remember, all else blurred until I found myself being urged to drink a large cup of railway tea heavily laced with brandy.

Twelve hours of such travelling, air raids, no food and then brandy are not really the best preparations to meet one's future in-laws. I remember only a mass of different faces, voices giving me good wishes, a hasty meeting with the vicar who would marry us and then the glorious comfort of my bed in a house from which Stanley had been banished for fear of bad luck should he see me next morning before our wedding. There were telegrams telling me that neither my brother nor Mary could get permission to travel, but I was too weary to feel great disappointment.

I think I felt more lonely than ever before in my life when I entered the church that day. Stanley's stepfather was to give me away, and we had set out together in a taxi to collect, on our way to the church, the wedding cake which the family had determined we were to have, wartime or not; they had saved precious rations for several months for this purpose.

The church was very dark and cold, because there was a power-cut. The flowers that I had ordered for the altar were there in place but still lying wrapped in the florist's paper (it was too dark for the guests to have noticed). There were friends and relatives for Stanley but not a familiar face to greet me. Happy as I was to be marrying Stanley, I did so wish it had been in that church near Bexhill. But the reception was a truly joyous one, for Stanley's sister, her husband and two young children had come safely back from West Africa, and his small niece had been delighted to act as my bridesmaid.

Soon we were on honeymoon in Edinburgh, walking the hills, seeing the sights. But all too soon it was over, and I had to leave him and return to my work.

Mary's parents were agog to hear all my news, though her mother was disappointed that I had no presents to show her. Most of my friends and family had sent us cheques – 'to buy a suitable gift when you have a settled home'.

A whisper reached me that I would soon be sent overseas again, and Stanley was detailed to a unit preparing for Europe and more minefields, I feared. Then his orders were altered, and he was sent to Ashton-under-Lyne. Meeting then was almost as difficult as it had been in Suez. Train services would not permit me to travel on Sundays and get back for Monday duty, and Stanley could manage only a halfday on Sundays. When we did try to meet, one or the other spent most of the free time in slow cross-country trains or buses.

Stanley wrote that he had met a senior QA matron who was lunching in his mess one day. She had asked for news of me, and after he had told her where I was stationed and that I had been warned of a posting to Europe soon, he had said he thought I had done my share of overseas work. It seems she had fixed him with an icy look before replying, 'You may be a very big noise here, Captain, but we QAs manage our own affairs.' After this letter I expected to receive a very sticky posting.

Soon after, I was told to report to a unit going overseas. I had packed my trunk and sent off letters and telegrams to Stanley and my family giving change of address, and then those orders were cancelled and instead I had to travel to Lincoln.

This hospital had been a sanatorium before the war, and the wards were connected by long walkways whose leaky roofs dripped smutty liquid whether it was raining or not. Every evening my medical patients laid bets with their surgical counterparts as to where the bombers were going, as wave after wave of them roared over our heads, and although they seemed to joke about it, most of them lay wakeful at night, willing those airmen to come back safely, waiting to count them in.

An air raid and those leaky roofs caused my next worries. Pulling beds across a ward is not the best exercise for early pregnancy, even if the patients are getting soaked by water pouring onto their plasters. The obstetrician hastily summoned from the town maternity hospital said, 'I am afraid you are going to lose this baby, Sister.'

We had talked long and hard about starting a family. 'How will you feel if I do not come through this war and you are left to bring up a child on your own? And is this really the right time for children to be born?' Stanley had asked.

'At least I would have something of you left to me. And is there ever a perfect time for a child to be born?' was my obstinate reply.

I stayed for a few days in Lincoln and was then sent on a long, bumpy journey by ambulance to Catterick Hospital. There to greet me were my dear friend Eve and that senior sister who once again called me 'her bird' and insisted I was looking peaky and that she would need to feed me up again on Guinness – which I had loathed – as she had when I was convalescent after malaria. It was so good to see them again, and as all now seemed to be going well with the baby, I was sent back to Lincoln.

A few more weeks of work and then more alarms about the baby. The medical prognosis was again poor, so I was not permitted to submit my resignation. I was given 'Compassionate Leave', so that if there were no baby I could be recalled to the QAs and not be claimed by other branches of nursing. I went to my parents' home, where, if my mother had her way, our nights were spent in an Anderson shelter in the garden, for buzz bombs were a frequent occurrence.

Stanley's unit was then moved to Berkshire, but there seemed little hope of army quarters for us. Suddenly someone in my family remembered some distant cousins living there. I had never met them, but that did not seem to matter in these strange war days, and after I had written and introduced myself, I was invited down for a weekend. And then I entered a new world.

They were two maiden ladies, by then in their sixties. All their lives had been spent in this sleepy old town where their father had had a shoeshop. Staunch members of the chapel, they had served in the shop, cared for their aged parents and later carried on the trade together. Everyone knew them, and they knew everyone. No one dared to sneeze without their knowledge, and they kept careful watch on the movements of all who passed their shop in the high street. They were like characters out of a book. But how kind they were to Stanley and to me! Wartime rationing seemed unknown to them. They had always had their own system of barter. They fed us on real country fare, produced butter, cheese and eggs for me to take home to my mother and lit a coal fire in my bedroom each evening. And above all, they found us a house – or a large part of one.

A friend of theirs had just lost the relative with whom she lived. A retired school teacher, she was terrified of having strangers billeted on her. 'They may be mothers with small children, bombed out in London; or someone has said I could be asked to take unmarried girls waiting to go into the nearby maternity home,' she had said, shaking at the thought.

Swiftly my two cousins prevailed on her to meet us. It would be far better, they advised, to take in an army officer and his wife who had been introduced to her, even though there would be a baby later. Still nervous, she asked us to 'take tea' with her. The rooms and the garden delighted us, and after the 'dear Major' had suggested that in future the mowing of the two lawns be left to him, we were warmly welcomed as tenants.

'Your nursing days are over, sweetheart,' my husband said as we sat for the first time in our own sitting-room with windows opened wide onto flower-filled beds.

He could not know that for him life would be short. That he would die of an illness aggravated by his service in the desert. That he would not live to watch his two daughters grow from childhood, see them married, hold his grandchildren. Nor know that I would return to nursing and work for many years among mothers and babies in Lancashire.

So many hospitals, so many patients, since those early stammering days when I met that first matron in her crisp white cap. And yet, through all the years, I never did wear those coveted strings.